# Behavior Modification
# With Children

## A Systematic Guide

Richard J. Morris
*Syracuse University*

Winthrop Publishers, Inc.
*Cambridge, Massachusetts*

**Library of Congress Cataloging in Publication Data**

Morris, Richard J
    Behavior modification with children.

    Filmography: p. 207
    Bibliography: p. 225
    Includes index.
    1.  Behavior therapy.    2.  Child psychotherapy.
I.  Title.
RJ505.B4M67    618.9′28′914    75–28101
ISBN 0–87626–073–3
ISBN 0–87626–072–5 pbk.

© *1976 by Winthrop Publishers, Inc.*
17 Dunster Street, Cambridge, Massachusetts  02138

10 9 8 7 6 5 4 3 2 1

*To Vinnie—a continuous source of love*

# Contents

*chapter 7*
## Problems and Difficulties in Starting a Behavior Modification Program    167

*appendix A*
## Behavior Evaluation Checklist    179

*appendix B*
## Record Sheets    189

*appendix C*
## Behavior Chart    195

# Preface

The research literature on behavior modification with children has grown at an exponential rate during the past five years. What has emerged from this literature is the well-documented view that many procedures now have sufficient experimental support to merit their utilization in less controlled settings, and that such procedures can be used quite effectively by teachers, parents, psychiatric attendants, therapy aides, and others who work with emotionally disturbed, mentally retarded, and physically handicapped children.

This book was written to assist those individuals who work with severely handicapped children in the use of behavior modification techniques. Its primary purpose is to present a detailed and systematic guide to the planning and implementation of behavior modification programs for children. Much of the book is based on a series of research-oriented training programs that were carried out with parents, therapy aides, special education teachers, and undergraduate students who work with emotionally disturbed and other handicapped children living in either institutional or noninstitutional settings.

The material is discussed in a nontechnical and readable fashion, and it is assumed that the reader has no previous knowledge of behavior modification or theories of learning. As a supplement to the text material, numerous examples of the use of behavior modification techniques are presented. Moreover, in order to maximize the reader's understanding and review of the material, chapter summaries are presented at the beginning and study questions are provided at the end of every chapter.

This book is written for a diverse audience, including students who are preparing to enter the (child) mental health and/or mental retardation area; nursing students interested in psychiatric nursing with children; parents; clinicians; and those involved with inservice training programs for psychiatric nurses, psychiatric attendants, therapy aides, and special education teachers.

Portions of this book were prepared while I was on leave from Syracuse University and was a Scientific Consultant to the Bavarian State Institute for Early Childhood Education, Munich, Germany. I would like to thank Dr. Wassilios E. Fthenakis, Director of the Institute; the Ministry of Education of the Bavarian State Government; and Syracuse University for making my leave possible.

Many people contribute a significant amount of time to ready a book for publication. Special appreciation is due Sherry Preisler for spending many hours deciphering my handwriting and typing the major portion of the manuscript. Appreciation is also due Sylvia-Inge Hanauer for typing additional portions of the manuscript, Donna Manaker and Elaine Morisano for critically reading the manuscript, and Kenneth R. Suckerman, M. Catherine Wheeler, and John H. O'Neill for assisting me in developing a number of the prescriptive programs discussed in Chapter 6. Many of these programs were first prepared during the conduct of research and the development of demonstration projects at the Syracuse Developmental Center, Syracuse, New York. I would like to express my appreciation to Dr. Theodore J. DiBuono, Deputy Director of the Syracuse Developmental Center, for making the children and facilities of the center available to me and to thank the various parents, teachers, and therapy aides who provided feedback regarding the implementation of these programs.

I also wish to express my gratitude to Paul E. O'Connell of Winthrop Publishers, and to thank Drs. Lee Meyerson and Nancy Kerr for being such outstanding role models during my graduate career and for stimulating my interest in working with retarded, autistic, and schizophrenic children. Finally, special thanks are due my wife, Vinnie, for her editorial assistance as well as her ever-present understanding, kindness, and support throughout the writing of this book.

Richard J. Morris
*Syracuse, New York*

*chapter* **1**

# Introduction

*In this chapter, we first briefly trace the history of therapy approaches with children. Following this is a discussion of the general assumptions of behavior modification treatment. This is followed by a presentation of those behavior problems that have been treated in severely handicapped children using behavior modification procedures. Closing the chapter are guidelines for the reader in the use of this book.*

## Overview of Therapy Approaches With Children

The formal treatment of children's behavior problems can be traced back to the early 1900s and the days of Sigmund Freud. Freud worked mainly with adults, and derived his therapy method (called *psychoanalysis*) from his therapeutic work with them. On occasion he did treat a child who was having problems. One of the first cases involving a child on which he consulted concerned a boy called "Little Hans." Hans was almost five years old and was very afraid of horses. His fear that one would bite him caused him to be reluctant to leave the house.

Although Hans's problem was treated successfully, it was not until 15 to 20 years later that Freudian psychoanalytic child therapy, combined with the play activities of children, was more widely used. Since therapists could not rely on the verbal communication skills of children, they introduced the use of children's play to help both the therapist and the patient understand and work through the child's problem.

Psychoanalytic play therapy was influential in the development of most of the later forms of child therapy. Two therapy approaches developed, however, which were quite different from psychoanalytic forms of therapy. The first treatment method emphasized the importance of establishing a meaningful relationship between the child and the therapist and deemphasized the Freudian approach of attributing unconscious meaning to the child's verbalizations and play activities. Therapy involved providing the child with a warm, permissive, and accepting environment in which there were few limitations placed on him, one where he could be himself and help himself reach his fullest potential of psychological growth and mental health. This general approach is often associated with Frederick Allen and Virginia Axline. They each developed a slightly different therapy approach, although both agreed that the child as a person should be the focus of therapy.

The second nonpsychoanalytic approach to develop, and the one which is the subject of this book, dates back almost as far as the Freudian approach. It emerged largely from the experimental psychology laboratory rather than from direct interaction with patients (as was the case with both the Freudian and relationship forms of therapy). This therapy approach became known as *behavior modification*. Behavior modification is based on theories concerning how people and animals learn to do various things, i.e., *how people and animals learn to behave*. A number of theories of learning have been developed by psychologists and tested in scientific laboratories over the past fifty years. Two general assumptions which have been repeatedly supported by the research are that people and animals behave in predictable ways and that there are principles which explain the manner in which they learn to do things.

On the basis of these principles, psychologists began applying what they learned in the laboratory to their understanding of the development and treatment of behavior problems in children and adults. One of the most famous early studies of the development of childhood behavior problems was conducted by John B. Watson in 1920 with an eleven-month-old child named Albert. Watson demonstrated that through the use of learning principles he could *teach* a child to become afraid of a white rat, and that this *conditioned (learned)* fear could be generalized to a fear of other animals and furrylike objects (e.g., a white rabbit, a dog, a piece of cotton).

A few years later, another psychologist, Mary Cover Jones, showed how learning principles could be used to reduce a child's fear of rabbits. Dr. Jones worked with a child named Peter. She successfully treated Peter's fear by pairing the gradual approach of the rabbit with the pleasurable activity of eating. In this way, she was able to demonstrate that a child's fear can be *counter-*

*conditioned (or unlearned)* using a procedure based on learning theory.

In this book we will concern ourselves with various behavior modification procedures, describing them in a nontechnical manner, in the hope that the reader will be able to apply these procedures to his/her children who have behavior problems or to the behavior problems of the children with whom he/she works.

## General Assumptions of Behavior Modification

Before discussing specific behavior modification procedures, we shall review some of the general working assumptions of behavior modification.

1. **Behavior problems are learned.** Although most scholars in behavior modification accept the fact that some childhood behavior disorders (for example, certain forms of mental retardation) are biologically or genetically caused, this does not necessarily mean that all behavior problems which are observed in children are also biologically or genetically caused. Similarly, just because we do not know the cause of a particular behavior problem or series of behavior disorders in a child, we do not have to assume that the cause is biological or genetic. The assumption which behavior modifiers make is that *a particular behavior problem in a child has been learned*—unless there is evidence to suggest the contrary. Thus, tantrums, bedtime problems, eating and dressing problems, throwing objects, isolate play, fears, and so forth are assumed to be learned by the child within the living situation.

2. **Behavior problems are learned separately.** Many children have more than one behavior problem—especially severely handicapped children. For example, a five-year-old child may not be able to eat completely independently, have a fear of harmless pet animals, and not be toilet trained. The assumptions that behavior therapists or behavior change

agents would make are that (1) each of these behavior problems was *learned* by the child, and (2) each behavior problem was learned separately from the other problems and developed independently. For example, there is no necessity for the behaviors we have mentioned to develop together. Any one or two of them could be present without the other(s). Unless there is *obvious evidence* to suggest that some of the behaviors were caused by a biological or genetic condition, behavior therapists assume the behaviors were learned, and learned separately.

3. **Behavior problems can be modified using behavior modification procedures.** A substantial amount of behavior modification research has been performed over the past twenty years on childhood behavior disorders. This research suggests that behavior modification procedures can be used effectively to change problem behaviors in children. This is not to suggest that such procedures represent "the answer" in the treatment of behavior disorders in children, but *the research does suggest that behavior modification procedures have wide application and merit consideration in the treatment of various childhood behavior problems.* Recent evidence even suggests that these procedures can be used effectively in the modification of some behavior problems which have an obvious physical or biological cause. For example, some researchers have been able to teach walking to children who have cerebral palsy or another physical problem which disrupts their coordination and the muscular development in their legs. Other researchers have been able to develop various social behaviors (for example, eye contact, imitative behavior, speech, and toilet habits) and control disruptive behaviors (for example, hitting others, making loud sounds, and self-hitting) in brain damaged children. This suggests that even if a child has obvious brain damage, some behavior problems can still be treated using behavior modification procedures.

4. **The behavior problems that a child shows in a particular situation indicate only how he typically behaves in that specific situation.** It is an obvious fact that children behave differ-

ently under different circumstances. A child may be a difficult management problem at home but a "perfect angel" at
school; a child may throw a tantrum to get what he wants
from his mother but never do so in front of his father; a child
may never feed herself when her mother is present, but feed
herself in front of a baby sitter. In each instance the behavior
problem or maladaptive behavior occurs *only* in a particular
situation. It is therefore assumed, unless there is contradic-
tory evidence, that a child's particular behavior problem is
specific to the conditions in which it has been learned and
does not generalize to other situations.

This is an important assumption because it forces the
change agent to look for possible reasons why the child has
learned to behave disruptively in the situation in which the
problem behavior occurs. That is, it helps the change agent
localize the possible reasons for the child learning to behave
in a disruptive or maladaptive way.

5. **Emphasis is placed on treating the child's problem in the
here and now.** Unlike certain forms of child therapy (e.g.,
psychoanalytic child therapy), behavior modification treatment focuses on what is *presently* contributing to the child's
problem, and on what can *presently* be done to change the
child's problem behavior. The emphasis is not on determining what developments in the child's early history caused his
present difficulty. *Emphasis is on the present* and on determining how the behavior can be changed in the situation(s)
in which it occurs.

For example, if a ten-year-old child is very aggressive at
home — hitting his brothers and sisters when he becomes
angry with them, destroying personal property of his parents
and/or siblings, and verbally threatening to get even with his
siblings and parents for what he feels they have done to
him — the emphasis of therapy would not be on determining
what occurred in the child's earlier years to "make him so
mean at home." Instead, treatment would be directed toward determining what factors in the child's present life situation are triggering these problem behaviors, and what can
be changed in his environment to modify the way he be-

haves. The change agent would not ask such *Why* questions as "Why do you feel so angry with your family?" and "Why do you feel everyone in the family is against you?" Nor would the change agent try to help the child identify events in his past which are presently making him so aggressive. Rather, *What* questions would be asked about the child and the family situation—for example, "What is occurring in the family right before Peter starts hitting his brother?" or "What occurs in the family right after Peter starts hitting his brother?" or "What can be changed in the situation to reduce the possibility of Peter hitting his brother?" After these types of questions are answered—given the assumptions which have been made so far—behavior modification treatment can be initiated.

6. **The goals of behavior modification are specific.** Since the orientation of behavior modification is toward identifying what can be changed in the child's environment to modify his particular behavior problem, it follows that the goals of treatment are specific; that is, the goal of each treatment procedure is to change a particular behavior of the child, rather than to achieve a more general goal of "helping the child get better" or "helping the child reach his highest level of adjustment." *A particular procedure is chosen to use in the modification of a particular behavior problem. The goal of treatment, therefore, is only the modification of that specific behavior.*

7. **Symptom substitution does not occur.** Some therapists believe that when the underlying problem is ignored and only the superficial problem (e.g., hitting or tantrums) is treated, the child will continue to develop new problem behaviors until the "deeper" issue is resolved. Although the question has not been totally resolved, the available research literature overwhelmingly indicates that new symptoms will not develop in a child when (a) the appropriate behavior modification procedure has been used and (b) there has been an accurate identification and modification of those factors which contribute to the child's behavior problem. If new symptoms do develop in the child or the old one(s) return, it

is probably because the same or similar precipitating factors which were in the original situation are present again.

These, then, are the general assumptions which underlie the use of behavior modification procedures. These assumptions represent a somewhat ideal position. In actual practice, not all people who use behavior modification procedures (whether they are psychologists, psychiatrists, counselors, social workers, teachers, attendants, therapy aides, or parents) agree with all of these assumptions. Their disagreement with particular assumptions, however, does not prevent them from using these tested procedures.

## Children's Behaviors Treated With Behavior Modification

Many types of childhood behavior problems have been treated using behavior modification. A list of some of these behaviors is presented in Table 1. While this list is not an exhaustive summary of all behaviors which have been worked with, it is a representative summary of those behaviors treated in severely handicapped children at home, in an institutional setting, in a therapist's office, or in a special education classroom.

Three categories of behaviors are listed in the table:

1. *Behaviors Strengthened:* those behaviors which a child does only some of the time. The change agent has to strengthen these behaviors (cause them to occur more frequently).
2. *Behaviors Developed:* those behaviors which a child does not perform. Here, the change agent typically develops these behaviors in the child and then strengthens them until they reach an acceptable level.
3. *Behaviors Reduced:* those behaviors which are judged to be inappropriate for the particular situation in which they occur. The change agent chooses a particular procedure with the goal of reducing the problem behavior until it reaches an acceptable level. In some cases the goal is to reduce the behavior to a lower level of occurrence and/or

**Table 1**

SELECTED CHILDREN'S BEHAVIORS WHICH HAVE BEEN TREATED USING BEHAVIOR MODIFICATION PROCEDURES

| Behaviors Strengthened | Behaviors Developed | Behaviors Reduced |
|---|---|---|
| Assertiveness | Arm/leg movement | Bowel movement in pants |
| Attending to educational tasks | Color discrimination | Climbing |
| Eating solid foods | Cooperative play | Constipation |
| Instruction/command following | Copying/tracing pictures | Crawling |
| Memory for spoken words | Echoing sounds | Destroying objects |
| Performing educational tasks | Eye contact | Fears |
| Playing with toys | Imitation | Fecal smearing |
| Question answering | Independent dressing/undressing | Fire setting |
| Sitting | Independent walking | Gestures with fingers |
| Social interaction | Making change | Headbanging |
| Speech articulation | Name discrimination | Hitting others |
| Spontaneous speech | Naming objects | Hyperactivity |

| Behaviors Strengthened | Behaviors Developed | Behaviors Reduced |
| --- | --- | --- |
| Talking to others | Reading | Loud vocal utterances |
| Use of eating utensils | Self-feeding | Overeating |
| Use of orthopedic devices for walking | Shoe tying | Pinching, biting, kicking others |
| Use of particular arm/leg | Size discrimination | Refusing to eat |
| Walking unaided | Smiling | Rocking |
| | Speech | Self-hitting/scratching |
| | Toilet training | Stealing/grabbing food |
| | Tooth brushing | Stuttering/stammering |
| | Tricycle riding | Tantrums, crying |
| | Using telephone | Throwing objects |
| | Washing face/hands | Thumbsucking |
| | | Tics |
| | | Urinating in bed at night |
| | | Vomiting |
| | | Yelling, screaming, hand-slapping |

teach the child to perform the behavior only in a particular situation.

Although this list does not cover all problem behaviors which have been treated with behavior modification procedures, it does suggest that a substantial number of behaviors have been changed using these techniques.

## How To Use This Book

This book is intended for use in work with severely handicapped children — whether the children are retarded, schizophrenic, autistic, and/or brain damaged. Since basic behavior modification procedures are presented, the book should first be used as a *resource book* to introduce the reader to behavior modification and the direct application of behavior modification procedures to children's problem behaviors. Secondly, the book should be used as a *reference volume,* not only for reviewing the use of particular procedures but also as a guide in helping the reader decide which method(s) should be used for treating a particular child's behavior problem.

The book should therefore be read first in its entirety (especially Chapters 1 through 5), and the reader should answer the study questions at the end of each chapter, as well as review the chapter summary *both before and after* reading a particular chapter. The study questions are intended to help the reader review the material presented in the chapters.

Chapter 6 should be reviewed in detail. In this chapter, the emphasis is on gaining an understanding of how and which behavior modification procedures should be used for changing specific behavior problems. Behavioral prescriptions are presented for changing particular childhood problems. These prescriptions are presented in systematic form, and should be used *only* after the reader has gained an understanding of the application of behavior modification procedures (Chapters 1 through 5) and the problems and difficulties associated with starting a behavior modification program (Chapter 7). The procedures are not difficult to use and do not require an extensive knowledge of psychology, but it is important to have a good "working knowledge" of these procedures before beginning a treatment program with a child.

## Study Questions

1. What are the three major forms of child therapy which have been used by therapists over the past fifty to sixty years? How do the three therapy approaches differ from each other?

(Review pp. 3–4 to check your answer)

2. Two important assumptions in behavior modification are that specific behavior problems are learned (unless there is obvious evidence to the contrary) and that such behaviors indicate only how the child behaves in a particular situation. Think about a particular child who has one or more behavior problems and try to determine how he/she might have *learned* to behave in this way. Are there some situations in which he/she *sometimes* shows this behavior, or *never* shows this behavior? If there are, why do you think that he/she has learned to show the behavior in some situations and not in others?

3. Review the list of children's behaviors which have been treated using behavior modification procedures. Are there some behavior problems exhibited by children with whom you work (or plan to work) that have been treated successfully using behavior modification? On a separate sheet of paper, write these problems down, and later in the book use this list to help you develop behavior modification treatment programs for these children.

4. What is the difference between *strengthening* a behavior and *developing* a behavior in a child?

(Review pp. 9–12 to check your answer)

*chapter* **2**

# Identifying and
# Recording Behavior

*In this chapter, we first discuss identifying a child's behavior problem — noting the importance of being very specific in stating what behavior needs to be changed. A discussion then follows on how to observe and count the behavior to be changed, as well as how to keep a chart on the child's progress. The chapter ends with a brief statement on making initial observations of the child's problem behavior and deciding which behavior should be changed first.*

## Identifying The Behavior To Be Changed

Before a behavior modification treatment program is started, we must first state what behavior is to be changed. This sounds like a simple task, and it is — once you learn the correct way to identify the behavior to be changed (often called the *target behavior*). In identifying a target behavior we are, of course, assuming that this behavior is learned and that it occurs because there are events in the child's immediate environment which encourage or allow the behavior to take place.

To help you in identifying target behaviors, look again at Table 1 (p. 10). This table lists a number of behaviors which have been changed using behavior modification procedures. Notice that each behavior is stated rather specifically — so that you or anyone else is able to know exactly what behavior was changed. Contrast these behaviors with the following list of behaviors which are not specific:

> Johnny should:
>> learn to have respect
>> not be aggressive
>> be cooperative
>> get along with other children
>> be good
>> not be so dependent
>> learn to dress himself
>> be gentlemanly (act like a gentleman)
>> not be destructive
>> be more independent

pay attention when someone calls his name
learn to do things on his own
be more polite
learn sanitary procedures
learn daily hygiene
learn to develop his physical potential
learn self-assertiveness
learn table manners
have a higher self-esteem
learn safety rules
learn recreation rules
learn to be polite

It is difficult to know exactly what behavior was to be changed in the child. For example, in the case of the proposed target behavior "Johnny should not be aggressive," we do not know if the therapist was interested in teaching Johnny not to hit others, not to kick others, not to push others, not to bite others, not to scream and yell at others, not to take toys from others, or not to pull the others' hair. Similarly, it is difficult to know exactly what was going to be changed in the proposed target behavior "Johnny should learn daily hygiene." Should the child learn to wash his hands, wash his face, brush his teeth, clean his fingernails, comb his hair, and so forth—we do not know for sure.

If you are not certain which behaviors need to be changed in a child, you should look at the *Behavior Evaluation Checklist* in Appendix A. This checklist lists a number of social, academic, and self-care behaviors which are commonly taught to children to help them progress developmentally. By rating a child as Always, Sometimes, or Never performing each of these behaviors, you will be able to determine some of the child's behaviors which need to be treated.

*In behavior modification programs, we must state specifically what behavior is to be changed.* Once this is accomplished, neither the therapist nor others who observe the child will be confused about knowing when the target behavior has or has not occurred. Instead of stating, for example, that you want Johnny to learn to stop being aggressive, you must state *precisely* what you want him to learn. Do you want him to stop hitting others, stop kicking others, stop throwing things at others, or what? Similarly, instead of saying, as in the next example, that Mary should learn to become more self-sufficient, we have to break down the behavior into more specific and observable behaviors.[1]

> Mary is an eight-year-old moderately retarded girl who attends a day school 5 ½ hours per day. Although she has progressed quite well in school and now reads and writes on her own, Mary's parents are very concerned about her "lack of self-sufficiency." Each parent tried separately for many months to help her become more "self-sufficient," but they failed and decided to consult with a psychologist about this problem. One of the psychologist's first tasks was teaching Mary's parents not to talk in general terms about what they wanted to change in Mary (namely, her "lack of self-sufficiency"), *but rather to state very specifically what they wanted her to learn.* Each parent had a different (although overlapping) idea about what he or she meant by Mary's "lack of self-sufficiency." After a number of tries at stating the target behaviors in specific terms, both parents agreed that they wanted Mary to learn to (1) button her blouse and coat, (2) tie her shoes, and (3) walk to and from the school bus stop by herself.

To Mary's parents, the absence of these three target behaviors meant that she was lacking self-sufficiency. To the psychologist, "lacking self-sufficiency" meant something else, but as soon as the target behaviors were specifically stated by her parents, everyone understood which behaviors were going to be modified.

To make sure that a target behavior is specifically and objectively stated, it should be able to pass the IBSO test (or, the *I*s the *B*ehavior *S*pecific and *O*bjective test).

## IBSO TEST QUESTIONS

**1.** Can you count the number of times that the behavior occurs in, for example, a 15-minute period, a one-hour period, or one

---

[1]Throughout this book the case studies and case examples have been modified to protect the anonymity of the children, parents, and therapists involved.

day? Or, can you count the number of minutes that it takes for the child to perform the behavior? That is, can you tell someone that the behavior occurred "X" number of times or "X" number of minutes today?

(Your answer should be *yes*)

2. Will a stranger know exactly what to look for when you tell him/her the target behavior you are planning to modify? That is, can you *actually see* the child performing the behavior when it occurs?

(Your answer should be *yes*)

3. Can you break down the target behavior into smaller behavioral components, each of which is *more specific and observable* than the original target behavior?

(Your answer should be *no*)

If the target behavior(s) you chose to modify fails any question on the IBSO test, you should redefine this behavior until your choice passes the test.

## Identifying Undesirable Target Behaviors

As a practice lesson to aid you in the identification of target behaviors, choose a child whom you feel shows undesirable behavior(s). Using the format in Table 2, list the *specific* undesirable target behaviors which need to be changed. Apply the IBSO test

**Table 2**
List for Identifying Undesirable Target Behaviors

| Situation Cues | Behavior | Behavior Should Be: Eliminated Reduced Restricted (*choose one*) | Consequences |
|---|---|---|---|
| | 1. | | |
| | 2. | | |
| | 3. | | |
| | 4. | | |
| | 5. | | |
| | 6. | | |

to each behavior on your list. Next show your list to a friend and ask him/her if he knows exactly which behavior(s) you are proposing to change in the child. If the behaviors pass the IBSO test and your friend feels that he could correctly identify this behavior without any ambiguity, you can be confident that you have objectively specified the target behavior.

Next to each behavior in Table 2, state whether you feel the behavior should be (1) eliminated completely, (2) reduced in the number of times it occurs, or (3) restricted to certain appropriate situations (that is, the child should be taught that such behavior is only appropriate in particular settings or situations).

Behavior modification assumes that a problem behavior is learned and, therefore, occurs because (1) certain environmental events called *situation cues* have stimulated the occurrence of the behavior and (2) other events called *consequences* have encouraged the repeatable demonstration of this behavior.

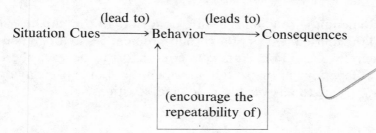

You should review your list now in Table 2 and write down the situation cues and consequences of each behavior. Some examples of situation cues and consequences for certain behaviors are the following:

| *Cue* | *Behavior* | *Consequence* |
|---|---|---|
| "Billy, it is time to go to bed." | Crying and screaming loudly | Mother/therapy aide says Billy can stay up longer and watch television. |
| "Susy, get dressed for school." | Susy takes at least one-half hour to dress. | Mother says, "Why can't you dress faster. You are always so slow," and helps her finish dressing. |

| Cue | Behavior | Consequence |
|---|---|---|
| Father reads at the dinner table and rarely looks at Davey. | Davey throws food at his sister. She screams. | Father puts down his paper and yells at Davey for misbehaving. Father does not return to reading paper. |
| George is watching a television program with no one else in the room. | George sucks his thumb. | Adult walks into the room and scolds him for acting like a baby, and tells him to stop thumb-sucking. |
| Bruce sees a dog. | Bruce cries and runs to his mother. | Mother comforts him and also says "Don't be afraid—everything is O.K." |

Sometimes we cannot easily identify both the situation cues and the consequences of a certain problem behavior. When this occurs, we should make a concerted effort to observe the child for a few days in the setting in which the problem behavior occurs, trying to answer the following questions:

1. What happens *immediately before* the problem behavior occurs? Does someone say something to the child which triggers the target behavior? Does someone come near him, hit him, or look at him? Is he working on a particular task (playing with a toy) and beginning to fail or show disinterest?

2. What happens *immediately after* the problem behavior occurs? Does the child receive exactly what he requested? Does someone comfort him or say something? Does someone move away from him? Does the problem behavior result in exactly what the child wanted to occur? (If so, what was it that he wanted to occur?)

If it is still difficult to identify the situation cues and consequences of the target behavior, we should then think about those situations or settings in which the target behavior does not occur. Specifically, you should ask yourself the following questions:

1. What is going on in this (these) situation(s) which does not take place in the situation where the child shows the target behavior?
2. What possible situation cues are absent in this setting but present in the problem behavior setting?
3. What potential consequences for the problem behavior are available to the child in the problem behavior setting that are not available in this setting?
4. What are the major differences between this setting and the problem behavior setting? Are some of these differences potential reasons why the problem behavior does not occur in this setting?

Some undesirable behaviors (e.g., nonimitative behavior, lack of speech, lack of toilet-trained behavior, not eating with a spoon) which a child demonstrates may not have obvious situation cues or consequences which encourage the repeatability of the behavior. Such behaviors may be due to learning deficits in the child which require that we redefine these undesirable behaviors in terms of *desirable behaviors* and then use behavior modification procedures to teach the child these desirable behaviors. For example, instead of saying that you want to eliminate a child's urinating in his pants, you redefine the undesirable behavior and state that you want to teach the child to urinate in the toilet. Or, instead of saying that you want to eliminate a child's eating food with his hands, you redefine this undesirable behavior and state that you want to teach him to use a spoon (a fork) to eat his food.

Similarly, there may be some undesirable behaviors (e.g., writing with a pen on walls, clothing, furniture, and paper; removing clothes) which a child shows that you do not want to reduce or eliminate; rather, you want to teach him the appropriate settings in which he should demonstrate these behaviors. These behaviors may initially occur in many settings, and he must be taught that they should occur only in certain settings. In such cases, as we will discuss later, the child has to be taught that the behavior can occur only when *certain situation cues* are present.

## Identifying Desirable Target Behaviors

Just as undesirable behaviors should be specifically stated, so too must desirable target behaviors. These behaviors can either be strengthened (increased) or developed in a child. By stating that a behavior should be *strengthened*, we mean that it is not occurring as often as we wish and we want to increase the number of times it occurs. For example,

> Billy is a four-year-old autistic child who eats occasionally with a fork or spoon and the rest of the time with his hands. The target behavior that his therapist chose to strengthen was Billy's use of a spoon or fork at mealtime.

When we want to *develop* a desirable behavior in a child, this means that the child is not presently performing the target behavior and he must be taught how to do it. In the next example, you can see a distinct difference between developing and strengthening a desirable behavior.

> Dicky is a 3 1/2-year-old moderately retarded child who does not eat with a spoon or fork. He occasionally eats with his hands, but he often demands that his mother or babysitter feed him. Since the parents felt that there was no obvious reason why he could not feed himself (and this was confirmed by the child's doctor), they chose as their target behavior developing independent eating in Dicky— first developing spoon eating and then developing eating with a fork.

There are some desirable behaviors which do not have to be strengthened or developed in a child. The child performs these behaviors adequately, but only in a few settings. Here the child must be taught to *expand* the number of settings or situation cues in which the behavior occurs. For example, some children follow commands, but only from one person—they "do not listen" to anyone else. Other children will use the toilet in their houses to have a bowel movement or urinate, but will not use a "strange" toilet—preferring to make in their pants. Still others will sleep comfortably in their own beds but will not sleep in a "strange" bed. In each of these cases, the child has to be taught to expand the number of situations in which he/she will perform the desirable behavior.

> Paula is 4 1/2 years old. She attends a normal preschool program and except for slowness in learning the alphabet and discriminating between colors, shapes, and sizes, she shows no signs of retardation or possible brain damage. The parents report few "out of the ordinary" behavior problems and feel that she is emotionally well balanced. However, they do report one major problem with her. Paula refuses to move from her crib to her "big bed" to sleep at night. She sleeps comfortably and undisturbed in the crib, but cries and has tantrums as soon as she is told that she must sleep in her "big bed." The parents chose sleeping in the "big bed" as the target behavior to expand.

Once again, think of a child whose behavior you would like to change. This time, using Table 3, list those desirable target behaviors which you feel he/she should demonstrate. Make sure that they are specifically stated and that each target behavior passes the IBSO test. Next to each behavior, indicate whether you want to strengthen, develop, or expand the target behavior.

**Table 3**
LIST FOR IDENTIFYING DESIRABLE TARGET BEHAVIORS

| Behavior | Behavior Should Be:<br>Strengthened<br>Developed<br>Expanded<br>(choose one) |
|---|---|
| 1. | |
| 2. | |
| 3. | |
| 4. | |
| 5. | |
| 6. | |

## Observing and Counting The Target Behavior

Once the target behavior has been identified and a decision has been made whether to eliminate, reduce, restrict, strengthen, develop, or expand it, the next step is to observe and count the behavior. Neither observing the behavior nor counting it is very difficult. But, in order to make sure that these activities do not occupy most of your time, it is necessary to develop an *observation plan* concerning when you should observe the occurrence or nonoccurrence of the target behavior.

Some target behaviors will determine *how often* you can observe the behavior; other behaviors will determine *in what way* you observe the behavior; and still others will determine both how often and in what way you observe the behavior. For example, if the target behavior is the elimination of food grabbing at the dinner table, you would observe the child each time he eats at the dinner table. If the target behavior is the development of imitative behavior, you would plan out daily observation sessions in which you would teach the child to imitate. And, if the target behavior is the strengthening of sitting in one's seat in the classroom, you would observe the child at selected times throughout the day.

Two types of observational sheets are often used in behavior modification programs. The first one is a *time-sampling procedure* and appears in Table 4. This procedure is used when (1) you are interested in knowing how often during the day (or part of the day) the target behavior occurs and (2) your plan is to strengthen, eliminate, or greatly reduce the occurrence of this behavior. When the particular observation time occurs, you observe the child for about 3–5 seconds and determine if he is or is not performing the target behavior. If he is performing the behavior, you place a "+" sign at that time period; if he is not performing the behavior, you place a "−" sign. The number of time periods you choose are determined by how often the target behavior occurs and the constraints on your own time. In addition, the observation periods need not occur at regular intervals; that is, you may want to try irregular observation periods—at some times every 15 minutes, at other times every 5 minutes, 10 minutes, or 30 minutes. This irregular procedure, however, can not be used in all cases.

In Tables 5 and 6 we present two additional examples of the use of this observational approach. Table 5 shows a sheet for observing a child's in-seat behavior on a regular basis. Table 6 shows an irregular time sheet for observing how often a child is playing in the backyard of his house (as opposed to in an alleyway).

## Table 4
SAMPLE OBSERVATION SHEET FOR DETERMINING THE NUMBER OF TIMES IN A DAY THAT A CHILD HAS DRY PANTS

+ = Yes, the behavior is present
− = No, the behavior is not present

Child's name:_____
Date:_____

OBSERVATION SHEET

| | | |
|---|---|---|
| 7:00 A.M. | 11:45 | 4:30 |
| 7:15 | 12:00 P.M. | 4:45 |
| 7:30 | 12:15 | 5:00 |
| 7:45 | 12:30 | 5:15 |
| 8:00 | 12:45 | 5:30 |
| 8:15 | 1:00 | 5:45 |
| 8:30 | 1:15 | 6:00 |
| 8:45 | 1:30 | 6:15 |
| 9:00 | 1:45 | 6:30 |
| 9:15 | 2:00 | 6:45 |
| 9:30 | 2:15 | 7:00 |
| 9:45 | 2:30 | 7:15 |
| 10:00 | 2:45 | 7:30 |
| 10:15 | 3:00 | 7:45 |
| 10:30 | 3:15 | 8:00 |
| 10:45 | 3:30 | 8:15 |
| 11:00 | 3:45 | 8:30 |
| 11:15 | 4:00 | 8:45 |
| 11:30 | 4:15 | 9:00 |

The second major method of observing a target behavior is during *scheduled* sessions. Here, one or two sessions per day or three to five sessions per week are planned with the child to observe how often the behavior occurs or does not occur. These sessions usually last between 10 and 30 minutes, depending on the target behavior and the tolerance of the child.

Implicit in the observation of a child's target behavior is counting how often it occurs. In behavior modification we do not simply get a general impression of how often the event occurred — we actually count the number of times it took place. This permits us to gain an objective understanding of how good, bad, or severe the child's behavior is.

In the case of the time-sampling procedure, we indicate at each time period whether the behavior did (+) or did not (−) occur and

**Table 5**

SAMPLE FORM FOR THE TIME-SAMPLING OBSERVATIONAL APPROACH ON A REGULAR BASIS

+ = Yes, the behavior occurred
− = No, the behavior did not occur

Child s name:_____
Week of:_____

OBSERVATION SHEET

| Day of the week | min. | Hour in the Day | | | | |
|---|---|---|---|---|---|---|
| | | 9:00 | 10:00 | 11:00 | 1:00 | 2:00 |
| Monday | 15 | | | | | |
| | 30 | | | | | |
| | 45 | | | | | |
| | 60 | | | | | |
| Tuesday | 15 | | | | | |
| | 30 | | | | | |
| | 45 | | | | | |
| | 60 | | | | | |
| Wednesday | 15 | | | | | |
| | 30 | | | | | |
| | 45 | | | | | |
| | 60 | | | | | |
| Thursday | 15 | | | | | |
| | 30 | | | | | |
| | 45 | | | | | |
| | 60 | | | | | |
| Friday | 15 | | | | | |
| | 30 | | | | | |
| | 45 | | | | | |
| | 60 | | | | | |

**Table 6**

SAMPLE FORM FOR THE TIME-SAMPLING OBSERVATIONAL APPROACH
ON AN IRREGULAR BASIS

| | |
|---|---|
| + = Yes, the behavior occurred | Child's name:_____ |
| − = No, the behavior did not occur | Date:_____ |

DAILY OBSERVATION SHEET

| | | |
|---|---|---|
| 8:30 | 9:50 | 1:45 |
| 8:40 | 10:05 | 1:50 |
| 8:45 | 10:35 | 2:00 |
| 9:00 | 10:40 | 2:30 |
| 9:15 | 10:55 | 2:45 |
| 9:20 | 1:00 | 3:00 |
| 9:25 | 1:05 | |
| 9:40 | 1:15 | |

then count the number of times the behavior occurred on that
particular day. For those target behaviors that are being taught or
changed during treatment sessions, we use a different counting
approach. Specifically, we use a simple tally sheet like the one
shown in Table 7. We indicate with a tally mark each time the
target behavior occurs and indicate with a zero each time the behavior does not occur. We then count the number of times that
the behavior occurred in that particular situation.

Sometimes we measure with a stopwatch instead of a tally
sheet, counting the number of minutes or seconds it takes the
child to perform the target behavior. The use of a stopwatch is
described in the next case study involving a young boy who was
slow in dressing himself.

Mark is a 6 1/2-year-old child who is very slow in dressing
himself. He knows how to dress himself and does not make
mistakes in dressing himself. However, he takes between
20 and 30 minutes to get dressed. Mark's mother chose as
the target behavior teaching him to dress faster. She counted
the number of minutes each day it took him to get dressed
by himself, starting the stopwatch immediately after he
finished breakfast and she told him to "go upstairs and get
dressed for school."

**Table 7**
TYPICAL TALLY SHEET USED IN BEHAVIOR MODIFICATION TREATMENT

| | |
|---|---|
| I = Behavior occurred<br>O = Behavior did not occur | Child's name: _Stephen_<br>Date: _11/17_<br>Time Session Started: _10:00_<br>Time Session Ended: _10:10_ |

SESSION TALLY SHEET

II O IIIII O II O O O O IIIII

II I I O I O O O I I I II O II I IIIII

OOO I I I I I II O O O I O O O I OOOO I

IIIII O IIIIIIIII O I I I I III

IIIII O O II O IIIIIII

Total Number of Target Behaviors: _84_
Length of Session: _10 min._

## Charting The Child's Progress

Besides observing and counting the target behavior in behavior modification therapy, we must also keep a chart of the child's progress. This chart enables us to know a great deal about the progress of treatment. For example:

1. Charting helps us readily determine the progress of a child's treatment in an unbiased and objective fashion.
2. Charting allows us to determine how regular the child's progress is, to determine whether the progress is steady or fluctuates.

The type of chart used in behavior modification therapy is presented in Figure 1. A chart, or graph, as used in behavior modification therapy consists of two major lines: the "Days, Sessions, Hours, or Weeks" line and the "Number of Times, Percent of Times, Number of Minutes, or Number of Steps"

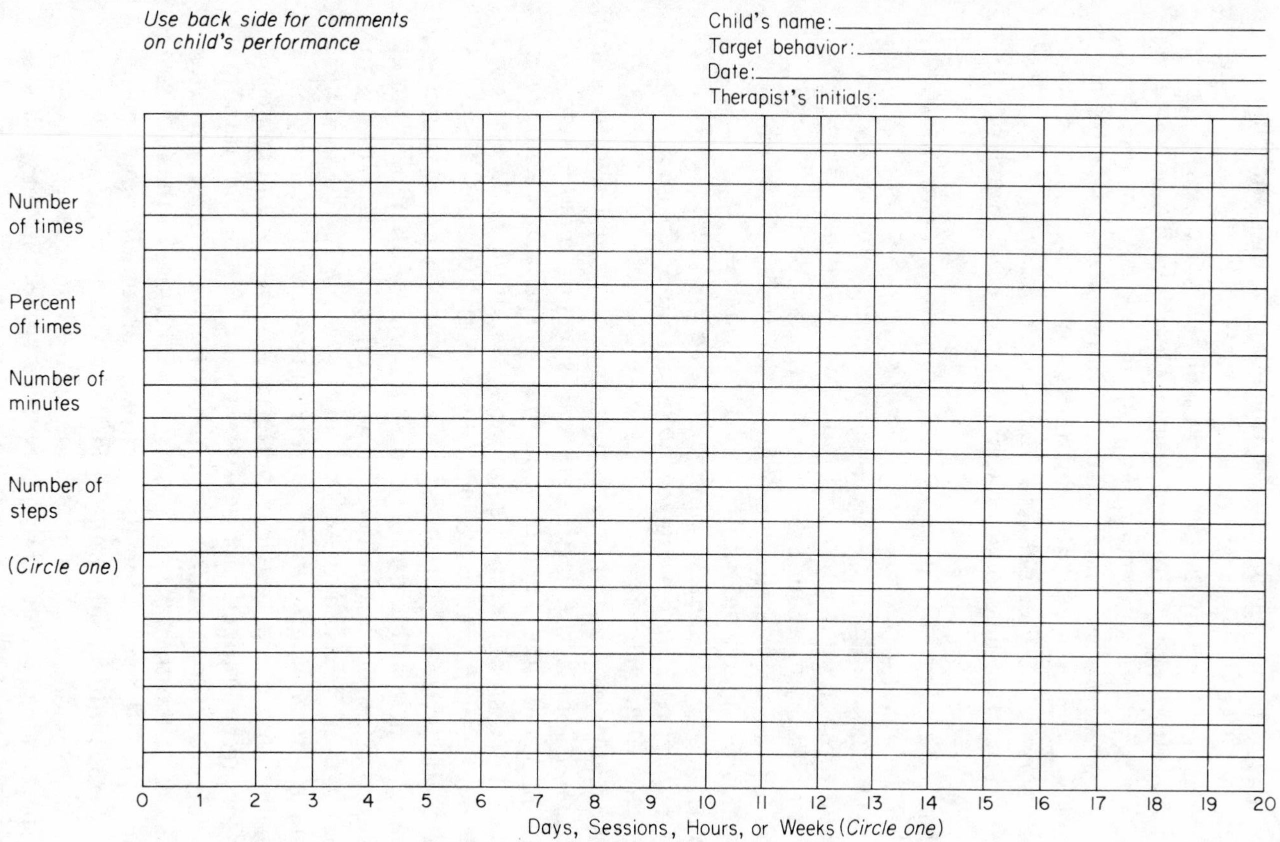

**Figure 1**

STANDARD CHART USED IN BEHAVIOR MODIFICATION TREATMENT.

line. The former is fairly straightforward—it lists the number of consecutive days, sessions, hours, or weeks in which treatment occurs. Most of the time, you will be recording the target behavior either per day or per session. Occasionally, however, a child's behavior occurs very often during the day. In this case, you may want to consider recording how often it occurs per hour and using a new chart each day. On the other hand, sometimes a child's target behavior does not occur very often. In this case, you would probably want to record how often it occurs per week.

The "Number of Times . . ." line *records how often the target behavior occurs in a particular day, session, hour, or week*. For example, if we were recording the number of times a child threw food at the lunch table, we would *first* count how often he threw food and, *second*, record for Day 1 the number of times the target behavior occurred. Thus, if he threw food 10 times we would record for Day 1 the number 10. This is accomplished by finding the number on the "Number of Times" line of Figure 1 and placing a dot where the ten line *crosses* the Day 1 line. This is shown in Figure 2.

We can also chart the percent of times a child performs a particular behavior. Charting percent is just as simple as charting number of times. Percent charting is especially useful when we are interested in knowing *how many times the child was correct out of a specific number of tries*. For example, Figure 3 charts the progress of a child (Jimmy) who was being taught to imitate what his therapist was doing. Jimmy's therapist would perform a particular behavior and then encourage Jimmy to imitate that behavior. The therapist was interested in determining Jimmy's *percentage correct* during each session. Since the therapist did not always perform the same number of behaviors to be imitated each session, it would not be fair to Jimmy to only record the number of times he was correct at each session. If the therapist performs 20 behaviors in the fifth session and 15 behaviors in the sixth session and Jimmy imitated 10 in the fifth session *and* 10 in the sixth session, we would never know that his behavior had improved unless we recorded his percentage correct. His percentage correct in the fifth session was 50% and in the sixth session was 67%.

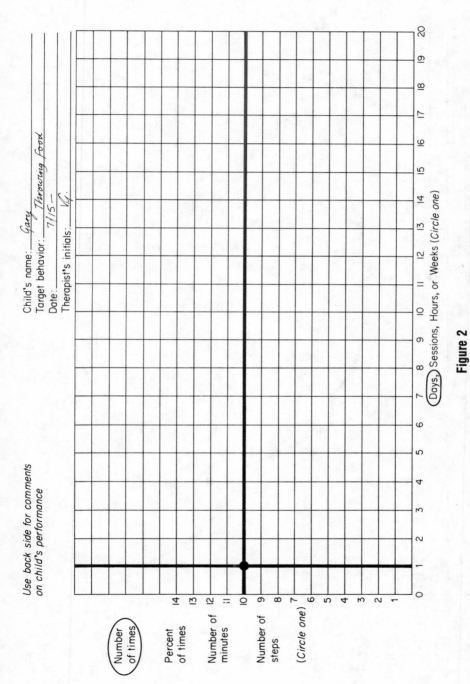

**Figure 2**

EXAMPLE OF HOW A CHART IS USED TO RECORD THE NUMBER OF TIMES A CHILD THROWS FOOD AT THE LUNCH TABLE.

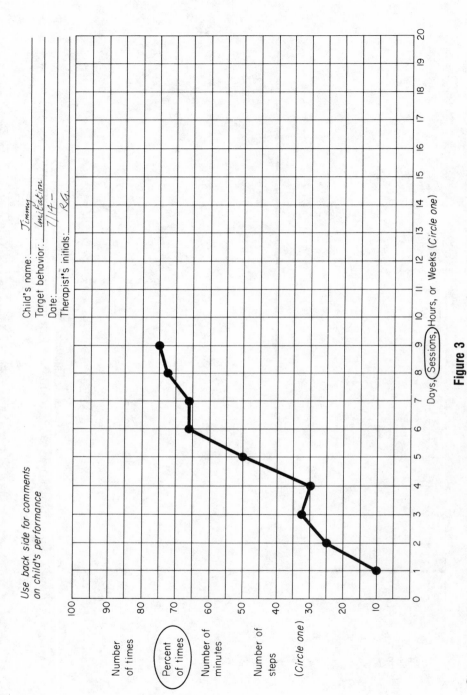

**Figure 3**

CHART OF JIMMY'S PROGRESS IN TERMS OF THE PERCENT OF TIMES HE WAS SUCCESSFUL IN IMITATING HIS THERAPIST.

*How do we calculate percentage correct?* It is not difficult:

1. Count the number of times that the child showed the target behavior.
2. Count the number of times that the child was requested to perform (or attempted to perform) the target behavior.
3. Divide the total from No. 2 into the total from No. 1.
4. Multiply the result from No. 3 by 100. This will give you the percentage correct.

An example of the use of these steps is presented in Table 8.

Finally, we can also chart the number of minutes or the number of steps completed. The "Minutes" chart is used when we are interested in knowing how long it takes a child to perform the target behavior. The "Steps" chart is especially useful when we are using a program such as those in Chapter 6. Here, *we record the last step that the child successfully completed* at the end of each session or each day.

Charting may seem complicated and time consuming at first, but *charting a child's progress actually takes very little time and provides the therapist with a clear, objective pictorial representation of how well the child is doing.*

After you decide whether you are going to record number of times, percent of times, number of minutes, or number of steps, make sure that you *circle the measure you are going to use.* Similarly, after you decide whether you are going to count the target behavior each day, session, hour, or week, make sure that you also *circle how often you are going to measure the behavior.*

### Table 8
EXAMPLE OF THE CALCULATION OF PERCENT CORRECT

Bobby imitates his therapist 50 times out of the 65 times that he is asked to imitate. What was Bobby's percentage of correct imitations?

1. Bobby imitated 50 times
2. Bobby was asked to imitate 65 times
3. Divide 65 into 50; 50/65 = .769
4. Multiply .769 by 100, .769 × 100 = 76.9

Bobby scored 76.9% correct imitations.

The next two cases illustrate some additional ways in which target behaviors are charted.

> Dennis is a seven-year-old moderately retarded child who is very slow in responding to his mother's commands. His mother never "pushed" him because she felt he could not move faster because he was retarded. She consulted with Dennis's teacher about his slowness and the teacher said that she had never noticed this problem. The mother then spoke to the school psychologist who suggested that she choose one particular command that she can ask at three different times during the day. She was then told to buy a stopwatch and to count how long it takes him to follow the command each time (that is, each session). She was to give the command only once each session.

Listed in Figure 4 is Dennis's chart for the first five days (or 15 sessions).

> Susan is a five-year-old hyperactive child who "can never sit still." Her mother told the psychologist that Susan's "nervousness" is particularly bad when she sits down to eat. In order for both the mother and the psychologist to determine how often Susan gets up from her seat, the mother was told to count for the next five days the number of times per day that Susan leaves the table during breakfast, lunch and dinner.

Figure 5 shows how often Susan left the table.

## Getting An Initial Impression of How Often The Child's Behavior Occurs

Now that you have read about how to identify a target behavior, as well as how to count and chart it, the next step we will discuss is actually observing and charting the target behavior. *This initial observation period occurs directly before you plan to start the treatment procedure,* and is called the *baseline period.* We establish a baseline in order to know how severe the target behavior is (or what the initial level of the child's target behavior is) before

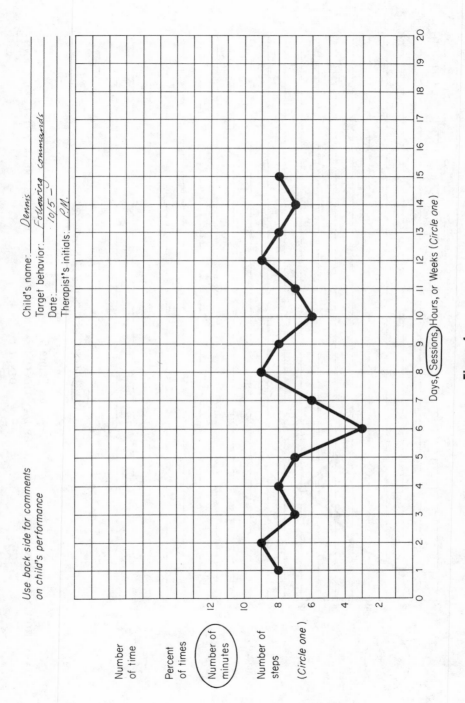

Use back side for comments
on child's performance

Child's name: _Dennis_
Target behavior: _Following commands_
Date: _10/5 –_
Therapist's initials: _P.M._

Number
of time

Percent
of times

(Number of
minutes)

Number of
steps

(Circle one)

Days, (Sessions,) Hours, or Weeks (Circle one)

**Figure 4**

CHART OF THE NUMBER OF MINUTES IT TOOK DENNIS TO FOLLOW A COMMAND OVER A 15-SESSION PERIOD.

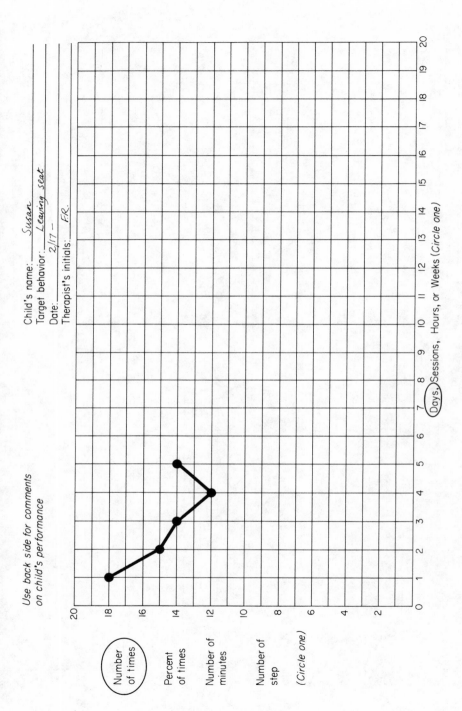

**Figure 5**

CHART SHOWING THE NUMBER OF TIMES PER DAY THAT SUSAN LEFT HER SEAT DURING BREAKFAST, LUNCH, AND DINNER.

we start treatment. This allows us to compare the child's progress during treatment to his behavioral level before treatment so that we know whether the treatment is having any effect on the child's behavior. Baseline information is especially important because sometimes we think a child is progressing with the treatment procedure when, in fact, his behavior during treatment is not appreciably different from his baseline behavior. If no progress occurs after a while, it is time to either switch to another behavior modification procedure or take a critical look at the procedure you are using to make sure it is being applied correctly. The baseline period should last five days, or between 5 and 15 sessions. Figures 4 and 5 represent baseline periods for Dennis and Susan.

## Which Target Behavior Should Be Changed First?

It is not uncommon for a particular child to have more than one target behavior which needs to be changed. The question then arises: which one first? To begin, you should list those target behaviors that need changing. The one you should change first is the one that you think would be *easiest to strengthen* in the child. This will give you exposure to working with behavior problems and also give you early feedback concerning how behavior modification treatment proceeds. It's better to know for yourself that the procedures work before you begin tackling more difficult target behaviors.

After you become familiar with the use of the various behavior modification procedures, you can begin treating more than one target behavior in the child. You should not try, however, to treat too many target behaviors within the same period of time. It is much easier to follow the progress of a few behaviors, and to remember what you should do whenever the behaviors do or do not occur, than to treat many target behaviors at a time and possibly forget what you are supposed to do.

## Study Questions

1. Which of the following target behaviors is/are not well defined? Circle the incorrect one(s).
   a. aggressiveness
   b. tying shoes
   c. spitting
   d. eating appropriately
   (Answer: a,d. Review pp. 17–18 to check your answer.)

2. Why should a target behavior be stated very specifically?




   (Review pp. 18–19 to check your answer.)

3. What are the three steps in the IBSO test?




   (Review pp. 19–20 to check your answer.)

4. What is a *situation cue*?




   (Review pp. 21–23 to check your answer.)

5. Choose a child whose behavior you would like to change.
   (a) What is the target behavior to be changed?
   (b) Apply the IBSO test to the target behavior.
   (c) List the *situation cues* which you believe lead to the target behavior.
   (d) List the *consequences* which you believe follow the target behavior.

(If necessary, review pp. 17–23.)

6. What do the following phrases mean?
   a. Strengthening the target behavior
   b. Expanding the target behavior
   c. Restricting the target behavior

(Review pp. 21–25 to check your answers.)

7. What is an observational plan? How is it used?

(Review pp. 25–30 to check your answers.)

8. Why should a child's progress be charted?

(Review pp. 30–32 to check your answer.)

9. Charles is an eleven-year-old severely retarded child who is being taught to imitate simple movements of his therapist.
   (a) In the first baseline session, Charles scored 3 correct imitations out of 45 demonstrated by his therapist. What is Charles's percentage correct?

   Answer: 6.6%. Review pp. 32–35 to check your calculations.

(b) Over the 10 treatment sessions, Charles scored the following percentages correct: 0,0,6.6,6.6,13.3,6.6,13.3, 20,20,40. On the chart in Appendix C (p. 197 ) record these numbers.

(Compare your chart to the one on p. 71. If necessary, review pp. 32–35.)

10. Why is it important to have a baseline period?

(Review pp. 36–39 to check your answer.)

*chapter* **3**

# The Use of Rewards

*The use of rewards in behavior modification with children is discussed in this chapter. We first review what a reward is and present examples of various types of rewards. A discussion then follows of the different ways in which rewards are given—for example, on a continuous versus an intermittent basis. Next, we consider those factors which influence the effectiveness of a reward. The chapter ends with a section on the use of tokens as rewards, and with a brief presentation of a few common misconceptions regarding the use of rewards.*

## What Is A Reward?

A reward is typically defined as an event which immediately follows a behavior and which results in an increase in the performance of that behavior. Thus, a reward is something which *follows* a particular behavior and *strengthens* (or, results in an increase in) the number of times that behavior occurs.

Since a reward is defined for our purposes in terms of its effects on the child, something which might be rewarding to one child may not be rewarding to another. Some children prefer to eat candy, popcorn, peanuts, or Crackerjack. Others dislike all of these things, but love sugar-coated cereals. It is therefore very important for the therapy agent to determine what is rewarding for each child with whom he/she works.

There are many ways of determining what is rewarding to a child. First, you could observe the child during mealtime, snacktime, and activity periods to see what he likes and dislikes— some children prefer candies over liquids, others the opposite, and still others prefer play activities over both candies and liquids. You could also ask the child what he likes the most and what he would prefer to receive as a reward. Or, you could use a *reward menu*. This menu lists by picture (and sometimes name) those major objects and/or activities the therapist knows the child likes. The child is then asked before each session which item(s) on the menu he would like to work for during that particular session. The therapist then uses those. Finally, you can give the child a preference test before the session begins. For this test, you need to have available three to six different types of objects and events which you feel the child likes. Then you systematically expose the child to each item (for example, you give him a few M&M candies, a few gumdrops, a drink of juice, and so forth) and determine which one(s) he prefers for that session. This last procedure is especially useful for those children who are nonverbal.

Following is a list of various types of rewards which most children enjoy:

1. Edibles (small bits of candy, teaspoonful of ice cream or gelatin)
2. Liquids (sip of Kool-Aid, juice, cola, lemonade, chocolate milk)
3. Objects (toys, pencil and paper, clay, whistle, bubble blower)
4. Activities (swinging, going on merry-go-round, running, playing catch)
5. Social praise ("Very good," "That's right," "Fine," "I'm so proud of you")
6. Nonverbal messages (smiling, tickling, hugging, kissing, rubbing back)

In Appendix D we present a more extensive list of possible rewards.

Now, think of a particular child with whom you plan to work. Using the previous list as well as the list in Appendix D, list three rewards for each of the categories mentioned which you feel will be potentially rewarding to the child.

## REWARD CATEGORIES

1. Edibles

2. Liquids

3. Objects

4. Activities

5. Social praise

6. Nonverbal messages

For some children, social praise is not a very effective reward, whereas food and liquids are quite effective. Even though praise is not a very good reward, you should plan to pair it whenever possible with the giving of the more effective reward. For example, you might say to the child after he has performed the correct behavior, "Very good," or "Good boy," and then give him his preferred reward.

*In general, no matter what reward you use with a child, be sure to praise him and let him know that you are pleased with him.* The amount of happiness and joy that you express should be slightly exaggerated in the beginning of treatment. Many severely handicapped children respond well to an adult's joy, enthusiasm, and concern over what they have done. Then, as the child begins to perform the particular behavior more regularly, you should gradually taper off your enthusiasm until it reaches a more moderate level. Here is an example of the use of slightly exaggerated joy and happiness to help an autistic child learn a simple matching task:

> Billy is a four-year-old nonverbal autistic child. He feeds himself, is toilet trained, and makes some discriminating sounds. The task of the therapy aide was to help Billy learn to point to a particular animal in a picture of five animals after seeing a toy figure of that animal. In one session, Billy was shown a horse and was then asked to "point to the horse in the picture." After a few unsuccessful tries, Billy pointed to the correct figure. The therapy aide jumped up, shouted "Hurray!" praised Billy, danced around in a circle with him, patted him on the back, smiled joyously, and gave him a big loving hug. Billy, who did not like candy or juice but liked to be hugged and have his back scratched, smiled and giggled and then sat back down with the therapy aide for another trial.
>
> The next time, a toy tiger was shown to Billy, and after studying the picture for a brief moment he first pointed to the wrong picture and appeared to wait for the excitement to occur again. When it did not, he then pointed to the correct picture. The excitement followed again.
>
> As the treatment sessions progressed, Billy became more skilled in identifying correct pictures and the therapy aide began gradually to decrease the activities which followed each correct response. The dancing around finally stopped as did the shouting of "Hurray!" but the aide continued patting Billy on the back and giving him social praise.

Occasionally a parent, teacher, therapy aide, or clinician forgets to reward a child for a correct behavior or does not remember what he/she is supposed to do when a child performs a correct behavior. One way of preventing this is to become very familiar with the treatment plan, but the following way is even better: make up signs describing what you are supposed to do when the correct behavior occurs, and hang them in various places so that they are easy to see.

For example,

PRAISE TOMMY WHEN HE EATS WITH A SPOON

Tell Susie How Happy You Are to See Her
Playing With Other Children

Praise Johnny Whenever You Notice Him Not
Pulling Someone's Hair

## Schedules of Reward

Up to this point, we have been talking about using a reward each time the child performs a correct behavior. There are instances, however, in which this continuous use of rewards is not preferable. In some cases the child may tire of receiving rewards and therefore perform the desirable behavior less often. Or the therapy agent may not have the time to reward the child each time the correct behavior occurs.

But even if it is possible to reward a child for each correct behavior, research indicates that this procedure may not be the most desirable. In most cases in which reward has been given continuously, the behavior rapidly decreases if the rewards are removed. This will *not* occur if, after the child is on his way to learning the target behavior, you begin rewarding him on an *intermittent* or *partial* basis instead of on a continuous basis. Continuous reward refers to the delivery of a reward after each time the child performs the target behavior; intermittent reward refers to the periodic delivery of a reward after the child performs the correct behavior.

The two most widely used schedules of rewards with severely handicapped children are the Fixed Ratio and Variable Ratio schedules.

FIXED RATIO REWARD SCHEDULE

In this schedule, the child receives a reward only after he has performed a *fixed* number of the target behaviors. The particular *ratio*—that is, the number of correct behaviors per one reward—is determined by the therapist and is based on what he/she feels is an appropriate ratio level for the child. Thus, a Fixed Ratio of four (abbreviated: FR4) means that the child will be rewarded after he has performed four correct behaviors. A FR6 means the child will be rewarded after six correct behaviors. An example of the use of a Fixed Ratio schedule is the following:

> Mrs. Martin was interested in teaching a mildly retarded child, Robin, how to discriminate between colors. She sat Robin in front of a series of rubber rings and two shoe boxes. Some of the rings were painted red and some were yellow; similarly, one of the boxes was red and the other was yellow. Mrs. Martin then told Robin to place the red rings in the red box and the yellow rings in the yellow box. Robin began sorting the rings.
>
> After the baseline sessions, Mrs. Martin introduced rewards for correct responding—each time Robin was successful, she received a lot of praise from her teacher as well as a piece of candy. Within 10 minutes of the first treatment session, Robin sorted all of the rings and was 40 percent successful. By the end of the third treatment session, she was about 80 percent successful. Mrs. Martin then decided that during the fourth session she would discontinue rewarding Robin on a continuous basis and instead reward her on a FR2.
>
> Robin scored about 80 percent again in the fourth session. The schedule was then changed to a FR3 in the next session and this time Robin scored almost 90 percent correct—obviously pleased with her successes and not affected by the schedule changes.

## VARIABLE RATIO REWARD SCHEDULE

This schedule is like the FR schedule except for one major difference: the child does not always receive the reward after the same (fixed) number of correct responses. A Variable Ratio schedule of three (abbreviated VR3), for example, means that the child will be rewarded on the *average* after every three correct responses. Thus, in one instance, he might receive a reward after he makes one response, at another time after he makes two responses, at another time after three responses, another time after four responses, and another time after five responses—but on the average he is being rewarded after every three responses. The particular arrangement of how many correct responses should be performed before each reward occurs is randomly pre-determined by the therapist. Thus, in the VR3 example, the arrangement of giving rewards could have been after 1,3,2,4,5 responses, after 3,2,4,5,1 responses, and so forth.

Two reward schedules which are not very frequently used in behavior modification work with severely disordered children are the Fixed Interval and Variable Interval schedules.

## FIXED INTERVAL REWARD SCHEDULE

In this schedule, the child receives a reward after a *fixed interval of time* has passed, but only upon performing the target behavior when the fixed interval has been completed. For example, a Fixed Interval of one minute (abbreviated FI1') means that a one-minute period must elapse before the child may have the opportunity to receive the reward; however, he cannot receive the reward until he performs the target behavior after the fixed interval period has passed.

## VARIABLE INTERVAL REWARD SCHEDULE

This schedule is like the FI schedule *except* the child does not always receive the reward after the same fixed interval. Instead, the child is rewarded on a variable time schedule which is randomly determined by the therapist. For example, if we set up a Variable Interval schedule of two minutes (abbreviated VI2'), this would mean that, on the average, the child is being rewarded after two minutes have elapsed. A child on this schedule, for instance, might be rewarded after 15 seconds, 45 seconds, 1 minute, 3 minutes, or 5 minutes—but on the average every two minutes. This form of interval schedule produces a steadier level of responding than does a FI schedule, and, as with the VR schedule, the particular times after which the child is rewarded are randomly established.

There is no particular rule regarding when you should switch a child from a continuous to a fixed or variable schedule of reward. The general rule of thumb is that once a child's behavior has stabilized and it seems that he/she has been responding at an acceptable level, switch him to a fixed schedule (and later to a variable schedule). His reactions to the switch will tell you if you have changed the schedule too soon or too abruptly. One way of avoiding any negative reactions to schedule changes is to make the changes in small gradual steps over a relatively long period of time.

It is important to switch a child eventually to a variable schedule, since this is the type of reward schedule which most often characterizes his interactions with his parents, teachers, and others in his life. When you are using, for example, ratio schedules, you should make sure that your schedule is not too thin—that is, be sure that you are not requesting the child to do too much work in order to receive one reward. The child will eventually stop responding correctly if he feels that the amount of effort expended is not equal to the payoff.

Lastly, *under no circumstances should treatment begin with the use of an intermittent schedule of reward.* Therapy should begin with continuous reward and then switched later to a fixed schedule (most often a ratio schedule) and finally to a variable (ratio) schedule.

## What Influences The Effectiveness of A Reward?

Now that we have described what a reward is as well as the various schedules of rewards, we will discuss briefly what influences a reward's effectiveness.

1. **Immediacy of the reward.** One of the most important factors affecting a reward is how immediately it is given after the correct behavior occurs. Researchers have found that as the interval increases between performing the correct response and receiving the reward, the effectiveness of the reward decreases. This finding has led to the following general rule: *A reward should be given to the child immediately after he/she performs the desired target behavior. Don't delay.*

2. **Combining praise with the reward.** Whenever possible, you should praise the child as you give him the reward. *Never give a reward without praise,* unless it is obvious that

the child does not like to be commended. Also, it is often a good idea to reflect your natural pleasure with the child's behavior—for example, smiling, showing joy and enthusiasm, and rubbing or patting the child on the back. Don't hold back your joy; show the child your happiness. Even when a child is on an intermittent schedule of reward, it is a good idea initially to praise him whenever he performs the behavior but does not receive tangible rewards (like food or liquid).

3. **Schedule of reward.** As we mentioned earlier, schedules of reward actually influence the effectiveness of a particular reward. The ideal scheduling of rewards begins with a continuous reward schedule. Then, after the target behavior appears to be moderately well established, the therapist should try out a low level Fixed Ratio schedule (e.g., a FR2 or FR3). If the child seems unaffected by this change and continues to respond at the same or a higher rate, the therapist should try out a slightly higher Fixed Ratio schedule (perhaps a FR5 or FR7).

If the therapist still meets with success, then he should try a Variable Ratio schedule (perhaps a VR2), then gradually move to a higher schedule as the child's behavior stabilizes. Variable schedules are the best for maintaining the child's motivation and interest in performing the target behavior. You can readily appreciate this last point if you think about the "one-armed bandit" slot machines in Las Vegas. The programming of these machines is based on a VR schedule of reward. Thousands of people play the slot machines every day for many hours to get just one jackpot (reward). The VR schedule these people are on maintains their motivation and interest in playing the machines (performing the target behavior).

A VR schedule also encourages generalization of a behavior, since the child learns that sometimes he will not receive a reward for performing the behavior while other times he will get rewarded. For example, if you are teaching a child to play and interact with other children, you would plan (after the behavior is established) to withdraw gradually from the situation and only appear every so often to reward him for his interactive play. The child would then be more likely to begin to perform the behavior not just for the tangible rewards from you but also for the attention and involvement he receives from others and the increased self-esteem he begins to feel.

4. **Type of reward.** Although it may seem obvious that the type of reward you give to a child will have an effect on his behavior, many people forget this fact. Some therapists, for example, continue to use the same reward day after day, session after session. Just as most people like variation in the type of food they eat each day, most children prefer variety in the types of rewards they receive. The best rule is to *use a reward menu or preference test before starting each training period.* Let the child help you determine which reward(s) he prefers for that particular session or day.

If the child seems bored during training or does not seem to be behaving with any amount of vigor, switch to another reward. Even if boredom or disinterest is not evident, it is often a good idea occasionally to alternate rewards within a particular training period.

5. **Quality and quantity of reward.** Sometimes a therapist forgets that candy, peanuts, popcorn, cola, juice, and so forth when left out more than a day or so can become stale and possibly spoil. *Be sure that you use fresh rewards throughout training.* Try the reward(s) yourself before a training period starts. If it does not taste fresh to you, do not use it with the child. Use a fresh supply.

How much you give a child each time he performs the target behavior is also important. Although a child may prefer a whole candy bar each time he performs a correct behavior, he would soon become "stuffed" and uninterested in doing more. It is best to *give edible and liquid rewards in small amounts, and activity and physical contact rewards for a correspondingly short period of time.*

For example, candy should be given in small bits. M&M-like chocolates are a good size for behavior modification work. One piece of this candy should be given for each correct response. One level teaspoonful of a reward is also a good size, e.g., a teaspoonful of ice cream, pudding, or gelatin. If you plan to use liquids as a reward, you should not give the child more than a few sips for each correct behavior. The dispensing of liquid rewards is discussed in Appendix F.

If, on the other hand, you plan to use activity as a reward, make sure that the activity period does not exceed one to three minutes—unless, of course, you are planning to use something like recess or a trip to the zoo as a reward for good behavior over a relatively long period of time.

6. **Who gives the reward.** To maximize the effectiveness of a reward, make sure that the child receives it from someone whom he likes and to whom he is attracted. In other words, *the reward should be given initially by someone who is a meaningful figure in the child's life.* After the behavior has become moderately well established, other people can be brought in to give the rewards so that generalization of the behavior to others can take place. If you plan to work with a child whom you have never met, it is best to first play with him for a few hours over a period of days. In this way, you can get to know one another, and you can become more familiar with the child's likes and dislikes.

## Token Economy System

It is unrealistic to expect a therapist to always reward a child with such things as candy, ice cream, pudding, juice, or cola. Moreover, some therapy agents do not like to give out such rewards. What would be better and perhaps more efficient would be a *symbolic reward system*, whereby the child could receive a reward symbol for performing the target behavior and then continue what he was doing without spending time consuming the reward. Such a system does exist. It is similar to our own dollar economy system, in which people receive symbolic paper (dollar bills) for performing various behaviors (working at a job) and then exchange their paper reward symbols for *actual* rewards (e.g., food, clothing, furniture, automobiles).

The name given to this type of system in behavior modification is *token economy system*. It is called an "economy system" because it is based on a "normal" monetary system. However, instead of receiving dollars for performing a target behavior, the children receive "tokens."

## WHAT IS A TOKEN?

Tokens come in all types and sizes. The following are examples of token reward symbols which have been used: gold stars, poker chips, metal washers, check marks or tally marks made on a sheet of paper, small pieces of colored paper, and plastic buttons. The common factor underlying all these tokens is that each is given in the same way as any other form of reward and all can be exchanged at a later time for an actual reward.

Although tokens come in different sizes and types, there are certain characteristics which all tokens and token systems must have:

1. A token should be something which the child can see, touch, and count.
2. The child must be able to store the tokens, or be able to go to a specific place to see how many he has earned.
3. The child must be able to exchange the tokens for actual rewards.
4. A child should not be able to obtain a token from sources other than the therapist or the therapist's assistants.
5. The child must know that a token can be exchanged for various rewards that he likes, and he must be able to know in advance how many tokens are needed to "purchase" particular rewards.
6. With the exception of check marks or tally marks, the token should not be so small nor so large that it prevents the child from handling it.

The tokens which children accumulate during therapy are stored in various ways. In some instances, the children keep their tokens in walletlike cases; in other instances, when check marks are used, the children carry a report card on which the therapist records each token they receive. In still other instances, tokens are stored for the children in a specific area to which they can go to look at or count the tokens they have received. For example, a child may have his tokens recorded on a poster which is taped to a wall in one section of his classroom, or in his bedroom at home or on the ward. There is no "best" system for either dispensing or storing tokens. It is best to try out different approaches to see which system best suits you and the child with whom you are working.[2]

## HOW IS A TOKEN SYSTEM ESTABLISHED?

The first step in establishing a token economy system is to identify what target behavior(s) you would like to change. Next, you should decide on the "medium of exchange" — that is, what particular item will be used as the token. Then you should choose the rewards which can be exchanged for the tokens. The rewards should include whatever items you believe the child would choose given an unlimited selection. Some examples of rewards used in token systems are:

Candy bar (small/large)
Chewing gum (stick/package)
Assorted pieces of individually wrapped chocolates
Bubble gum
Comic book; picture book
Bicycle ride
Watching television (varying length of time)
Listening to favorite record(s) (varying length of time)
Private use of transistor radio (with earphones)
   (varying length of time)
Private play time with therapist or other significant
   person (varying length of time)
Assorted jewelry
Assorted toiletries
Trips to home, zoo, museum, park, etc.
Different sized dolls
Toys
Games

---

[2]For those therapists who choose stars or check (and tally) marks, it is often helpful to let the child place or record his own token on the chart. If the child has difficulty in doing this, the therapist should help him out by guiding his hand.

Rewards can also be chosen from lists like the one presented in Appendix D. In addition, you can ask the child which "things" he would like to have.

After the target behavior(s) and the rewards are chosen, the next step is to price the rewards. Pricing is very subjective, although there are a few general guidelines which should govern how you price each item. First, the greater the supply of an item, and the less its cost to the therapist, the lower should be the price. However, supply is also affected by demand. If demand for a particular item is high (even if the supply is great), you may want to consider raising its price. Secondly, those items which require more of the therapist's time (e.g., going for a walk with the child) should have a higher price than those items requiring less therapist time. However, if demand for these latter items is low (and the therapist feels they are important for the child to have), then their price should be lowered.

Similarly, those items which are fewer in number (in terms of actual relative availability) should also be priced higher. Finally, if the child continues to purchase one or two items and the therapist feels that he should choose other items, then a revaluation of the items should take place in which the high demand items are increased in price and the low demand items are decreased in price or are maintained at the same price level.

Once the prices are set, it is often a good idea to watch closely in the beginning how the spending proceeds. Then, if changes are necessary, they can be made without much difficulty or delay. *A token-reward system should not be too lean or too fat.* The child should have an opportunity to buy something very small with one token, something great with many tokens, or something "nice" (but not great!) for an in-between number of tokens.

In dispensing the tokens, the therapist should give them in the same way he/she would give any other reward. That is, the child should be praised for good behavior and then given the token (i.e., the token should either be given to the child, placed in the child's "wallet," or recorded on a card so he can see it). *It is important to give a token with the same amount of enthusiasm as you would give other rewards.*

Initially, the child should be guided through the exchange system. For example, right after he makes the first few correct responses and is given his tokens, he should be brought to the exchange area and assisted in buying particular items. This introductory phase should be continued until the child learns what he is supposed to do. After this phase, the exchange should be "opened" at the end of each session (or even twice a day, depending on how many tokens are being earned). You may even find that because of the child's spending pattern you need to open the exchange only two or three times per week. Whatever the number of times that the exchange is opened each week, make sure that the child has enough time to buy things. Don't hurry him, but don't encourage dawdling either.

IS A TOKEN SYSTEM THE BEST APPROACH?

A token economy system is the preferred system of reward giving when you have to work with a group of children, whether in a classroom situation, in a home, or in an institutional setting. It is also a good system to use when there are many behaviors which you want the child to learn, and when you do not want to carry around an entire selection of rewards for the child. Token economy systems, however, are not for every child. Some children cannot adapt to the exchange system or learn to tolerate the delay in receiving a reward. Others may be too severely handicapped. But the only way to find out if the child you are working with will adapt to this system is to try it out. If it does not work, then go back to the tangible reward system and try the token-reward system again at a later time.

## Misconceptions About Rewards

One of the most common statements which many therapy agents make regarding the use of reward is that "Rewarding a child is nothing but bribery." This is just not true. "Bribery" is used to encourage or provide incentive to someone to perform an activity which is defined as illegal or deviant by society. Reward, on the other hand, is used to help a child perform an activity which is not viewed as either illegal or deviant by society. In fact, the behavior we are typically trying to teach the child is, in most instances, one which society values highly and encourages. Secondly, "bribery" typically occurs *before* the desirable behavior takes place (e.g., giving a policeman money so he will not write out your speeding ticket), whereas reward occurs *after* the desirable behavior takes place.

Often, one also hears the statement, "Why should I reward a child for something which he is supposed to do (or, is his duty to do)?" Without forging into a philosophical discussion regarding what one is *supposed* to do or what is one's *duty,* let us just say that we all are rewarded for doing things: we are rewarded with a salary for working, we are rewarded with a smile, a kiss, or a "Thank you" for helping other people or for being nice to others, and we are rewarded by our supervisors or boss at work for doing a good job. There is no reason we should not treat a child in the same way. Just as rewards maintain much of our adult behavior, so should rewards be used to strengthen or develop a child's behavior.

The proper use of rewards is a very effective component of teaching children desirable behaviors. But rewards have limits. No matter how attractive a reward is to a child, it will not be useful unless the child is developmentally and physically ready to perform the target behavior.

## Study Questions

1. What is a reward? What is a reward menu?

   (Review pp. 45–46 to check your answer.)

2. List the six types of rewards.
   a.
   b.
   c.
   d.
   e.
   f.
   (Review pp. 46–47 to check your answer.)

3. What should *always* be paired with the giving of a reward?

   (Review pp. 47–48 to check your answer.)

4. How does a continuous reward schedule differ from a variable reward schedule?

   (Review p. 49 to check your answer.)

5. How does a FR3 schedule of reward differ from a VR3 schedule?

   (Review pp. 49–51 to check your answer.)

6. List the six factors that influence the effectiveness of a reward.
   a.
   b.
   c.
   d.
   e.
   f.
   (Review pp. 52–55 to check your answer.)

7. How does a token economy system work?

   (Review pp. 55–59 to check your answer.)

8. List five characteristics which all tokens should have.
   a.
   b.
   c.
   d.
   e.
   (Review p. 56 to check your answer.)

9. How are the prices in a token economy system established?

   (Review p. 58 to check your answer.)

10. How does bribery differ from the application of rewards?

    (Review pp. 59–60 to check your answer.)

chapter 4

# Teaching
# Desirable Behaviors
# to Children

*In this chapter we discuss various procedures for teaching desirable behaviors to children. An outline for developing a treatment plan for a child is first presented. This is followed by a discussion of how to strengthen a desirable behavior and a presentation of some case examples involving the use of this procedure. Next, we discuss how to develop a new behavior in a child and again present some case examples. The use of behavioral chaining and modeling procedures is also reviewed, followed by a brief discussion of some of the potential problems in conducting a behavior modification program.*

## Developing A Treatment Plan

We learned in Chapter 1 that problem behaviors are assumed to be learned, and that these behaviors occur when certain situation cues are present and when particular consequences follow the behavior. We also learned that a child's behavior is very much influenced by what happens to him immediately after he performs the behavior. Thus, if a child's behavior leads to satisfying (or rewarding) consequences, we usually find that this behavior will be repeated whenever the same situation cues are present. This principle can be diagramed in the following way:

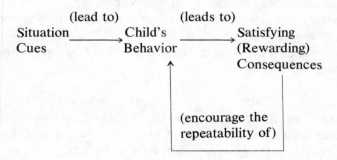

The first step in beginning a behavior modification procedure involves the formulation of a *treatment plan*. At first this may seem complicated, but it really is not. Listed in the following outline are the primary questions which should be answered in the formulation of a treatment plan involving the teaching of desirable behaviors. The purpose of the plan is to help the therapist delineate *exactly* what he/she will be doing before therapy begins, so that the therapist is completely prepared to work with the child.

## OUTLINE FOR DEVELOPING A TREATMENT PLAN

1. What is the desirable target behavior?
2. What method of observation am I going to use?
3. What am I going to chart?
   a. Circle one:
      Number of times
      Percent of times
      Number of minutes
      Number of steps
   b. Circle one:
      Sessions
      Days
      Hours
      Weeks
4. How long will the baseline phase be?
5. What is my criterion for success?
6. What will I *specifically* do when my child (the child I am working with) makes a correct response?
7. What will I *specifically* do when my child makes an incorrect response?
8. Any additional comments about the treatment procedure?

Questions 6, 7, and 8 define what the treatment plan will be. You should be able to answer each of these questions after you have read through this chapter. Question 5 is a somewhat subjective question. Its answer is determined by what is expected of the child by society as well as by your expectations and desires concerning the child. If, for example, I am interested in teaching a child to be imitative, I might set as my "criterion for success" 80 percent or above correct imitations for at least three consecutive sessions. Someone else who works with the child may set as his criterion 100 percent correct imitations for one session, and a third therapist may use the criterion of 90 percent or above correct imitations for two sessions. In all cases the criterion is much greater than 50 percent, but how much greater and the extent of mastery are subjective determinations.

Once a treatment plan has been formulated, you are ready to begin treatment.

## Strengthening A Desirable Behavior

Much of the therapy work with severely handicapped children involves the use of rewards to strengthen a child's target behavior. Presented here are a few case examples describing how rewards are used to strengthen a particular behavior. In the first case, different schedules of reward are used to modify the child's reluctance to look at people when they are near him or talking to him.

> Mark is an eight-year-old retarded youngster who shows signs of minimal brain damage. He is verbal, toilet trained, and moderately imitative. One problem which Mark's teacher has been unable to change involves his reluctance to look at people when they are interacting with him, whether they are talking to him or playing with him. His teacher, Mrs. Neal, chose eye contact as the target behavior to change. Since she was interested in teaching Mark to look at people in response to their playing with and/or talking to him, she decided not to teach him eye contact in response to an instruction to do so. Rather, she was more interested in strengthening his spontaneous eye contact with people.
>
> She observed Mark over a one-week period, two times per day, during a 10-minute free-play period, and counted the number of times that he looked at another child or adult. The target behavior was specifically defined as Mark looking at another person for three seconds.
>
> When the 10-session baseline period was over, Mrs. Neal decided to walk over to Mark each time she saw him glance at another person and say, "Good boy. You are looking at

other people. That's great." Then she would give him an M&M candy. By the fifteenth treatment session, Mark was looking at other people much more often than he did during baseline.

Mrs. Neal then decided to switch Mark to a FR3 schedule to see if he would continue to respond at a high level. He did, and by the end of the twentieth session his spontaneous eye contact was even higher than before. Mark then became sick and did not return to school for six days. Upon his return he was continued on the FR3 schedule for three days, but Mrs. Neal discovered that his eye contact had dropped down significantly from the previous week.

Mrs. Neal returned to a continuous reward schedule in order to raise the eye contact level again. Mark's eye contact rose rapidly, and within four more sessions he was back to his previous high level and back on a FR3 schedule. On the thirtieth session, Mrs. Neal switched him to a VR3 schedule with no ill effects over the next 10 sessions. By the fortieth session, treatment was discontinued. Mark was looking at others more frequently now and Mrs. Neal was very pleased with his progress.

In the next case, a schizophrenic child named Johnny is taught not to ride his tricycle into the street.

Johnny is a five-year-old boy who says a few words clearly and mumbles many others. He shows few, if any, aggressive tendencies, is moderately imitative, and is toilet trained. Recently, Mr. and Mrs. Wilkins bought Johnny a tricycle. Johnny was very pleased with the gift and rode it often. One day, Mrs. Wilkins noticed Johnny riding the tricycle in the street. She immediately ran outside, scolded him, and told him not to do that again.

Upon her return to the house, Mrs. Wilkins saw Johnny riding into the street again. She ran outside, removed him from the tricycle, and brought him into the house—forbidding him to go outside for the rest of the day. Although few cars traveled on the Wilkins's street, the possible danger to Johnny was obvious.

The next day, Johnny repeated his riding into the street despite firm warnings from both parents, and he continued this activity every day until Mrs. Wilkins had to keep him inside all the time. Concerned about his safety and the frustration Mrs. Wilkins felt about her inability to control her son, the parents spoke to a psychologist.

The psychologist and the Wilkinses came to the conclusion that Johnny was behaving in this way in order to get his mother's attention. The psychologist advised the Wilkinses to estimate how many times per day, if given the chance, Johnny would ride his tricycle into the street. (This form of baseline was arranged because of the danger involved in running a true baseline.) He then told the Wilkinses to go outside and observe Johnny playing every five minutes. If he was riding his tricycle on the sidewalk, Mr. or Mrs. Wilkins was to go up to him and praise him for riding his tricycle in the correct place and then give him a piece of his favorite candy.

If, on the other hand, he was on the street with the bike, he was to be brought into the house immediately in a matter-of-fact way and told that he could not go out for two hours. The number of times that Johnny rode into the street decreased sharply within a one-week period. Mrs. Wilkins then extended her observation time to every 10 minutes, and finally every 15 minutes. Three weeks later, Johnny no longer rode his tricycle into the street. As a result of Johnny's changed behavior, Mr. and Mrs. Wilkins spent much more time with him during his playtime outside.

Next, we see how *prompting* is used along with rewards to help strengthen a desirable behavior. Prompting involves the gradual assisting of a child in performing the desired target behavior until he learns what is expected of him. When he reaches this point of understanding, the prompts are then slowly withdrawn and the child is encouraged to perform the behavior on his own.

Jerry is a seven-year-old severely retarded child who is non-verbal, minimally imitative, and not toilet trained. The target behavior that his therapist chose to teach Jerry was imitative behavior. Using the program presented in Chapter Six, the therapist ran five baseline sessions with Jerry. Before she performed each behavior, she said, "Jerry, do this." She ran three trials per session, and each session lasted about 10 minutes.

Since Jerry's baseline imitative level was low, Miss Thomas decided to prompt each of the to-be-imitated behaviors so Jerry could learn what was expected of him. For example, after Miss Thomas raised her arms out to the sides and requested Jerry to do the same, she saw that Jerry did not imitate her. She then placed her hands under his arms and gently lifted them out to his sides. After prompting each response, Miss Thomas said, "Good boy," and rewarded him for performing the behavior. None of the prompted behaviors, however, were recorded as a success on Jerry's chart.

After eight sessions of prompting almost every response, Jerry began to show signs of learning what to do. Consequently, Miss Thomas began to withdraw her prompts, and Jerry began imitating Miss Thomas's movements in response to the command "Jerry, do this." He was soon imitating at a much higher rate than during baseline. By the twentieth session, as you can see in Figure 6, Jerry was correctly responding 60 percent of the time. By the thirty-fifth session (not shown), he was responding correctly 90 percent of the time.

As you can see from these three examples, the use of rewards is a powerful way to strengthen a target behavior. But sometimes, as in this final case example, rewards can be used inappropriately.

Mrs. James was quite upset because all her attempts over a three-year period had failed to "train" eight-year-old Howard to keep his thumb out of his mouth. She had tried scolding him whenever he sucked his thumb, removing privileges each time she "caught" him, bandaging the thumb or putting pepper on it (leading him to suck his index finger!), and other methods. Each method had failed. One day she read about reward procedures.

The next day, she began observing more regularly and started rewarding him with candy each time she saw him take his finger out of his mouth. She did this for three weeks. The only result was that Howard received a lot of candy and praise for removing his finger, and was never scolded for thumbsucking. But he still sucked his thumb very often.

Mrs. James contacted a psychologist who told her what

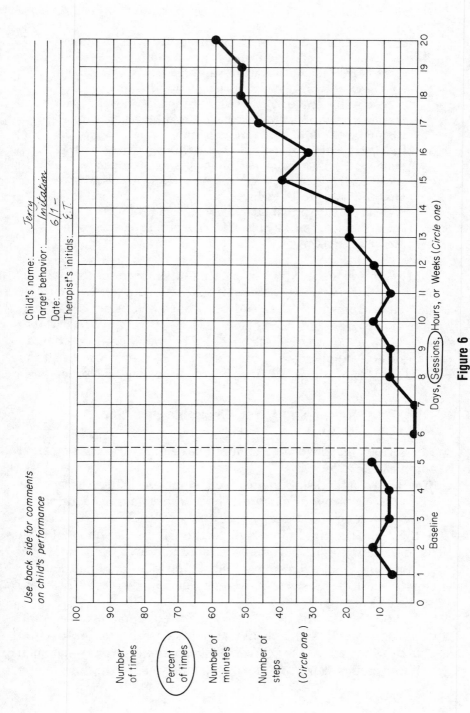

**Figure 6**

CHART SHOWING JERRY'S PROGRESS IN LEARNING TO IMITATE SIMPLE BEHAVIORS.

she was doing wrong. He praised her for trying the new technique but pointed out that her procedure had no effect on Howard's thumbsucking because the *only* way he could receive a reward was by first sucking his thumb.

Since Howard only sucked his thumb when he was watching television, the psychologist told Mrs. James to begin a program of only rewarding Howard when he was not sucking his thumb and not say anything when he was thumbsucking. She followed this suggestion for three weeks and then reported back to the psychologist. She said that Howard had "greatly reduced" his thumbsucking and took pride in telling her that he had not sucked his thumb for an entire evening. One month later, she reported that he was no longer thumbsucking.

From this example you can see that it is important that you do not reward the wrong behavior. If you choose a particular treatment approach with a child and you notice that after 5 or 10 sessions no progress has been made, review your approach in detail and check to see that you are rewarding the appropriate behavior, correctly applying the procedure, and using a reward that the child likes. If progress still does not occur, change the procedure.

## Developing A New Desirable Behavior

For various reasons, some children have difficulty learning such complex behaviors as tying shoes, eating with a spoon or fork, dressing or undressing themselves, color and name discrimination, how to throw or catch a ball, toothbrushing, and zipping a jacket. Although the therapy agent tries to teach these behaviors to the child, the child often fails to learn the skill and soon both he and the therapist become frustrated and give up. Sometimes the therapy agent even says to himself or to others that the child cannot learn because he is too retarded or disturbed or brain damaged.

Although it may be true that some severely handicapped children cannot learn some behaviors because the behaviors are too complex for their mastery level, it is also often the case that such children cannot learn complex behaviors because they are taught all parts of the behavior at once rather than being taught parts of the behavior separately. In most cases, in order to develop a new behavior in a child it is necessary to divide the behavior into its component parts and teach each part consecutively until the child learns the whole complex behavior. This procedure is especially important to follow when you plan to teach a child various social and self-help skills.

## HOW TO TEACH A NEW BEHAVIOR

If you look back to Table 1 in Chapter 1, you will notice that many behaviors (some quite complex) have been taught to severely handicapped children. Although the particular target behaviors differ, the same teaching principle underlies the learning process. This principle, often called *successive approximation* or *shaping*, states that the child should be taught a complex activity in successive steps—with each step gradually leading to an approximation of the desired target behavior.

For example, instead of teaching a child the whole behavior of putting on a pair of pants, we would instead break up this complex behavior into its component parts. The parts would then be arranged in gradual successive steps, leading to the final step of pulling up one's pants. Here are the preliminary steps involved in learning to put on one's pants:

1. Pull pants up from just below waist. (Use loose-fitting pants which have an elasticized waistband, no buttons, and no zipper.)
2. Pull pants up from hip region.
3. Pull pants up from knees.
4. Have child sit down with pants up to knees. Then have him stand up and pull pants up from knees.
5. Have child sit down with pants just over feet (by the ankles). Have child pull pants to knees, and then stand up and pull pants all the way up.
6. Have child sit down with pants just over toes. Have child pull pants to knees, and then stand up and pull pants all the way up.

7. Have child sit down. Place one of child's feet into one of the pant legs until his toes show. Then have child place his other foot through the other pant leg and pull the pants to his knees. Then have him stand up and pull the pants all the way up.

8. Have child sit down. Place pants in front of child with the opening of one pant leg just touching the toes of one foot. Have him pull the pant leg up until his toes show. Then have him place his second foot in the other pants leg. Then have him pull the pants up to his knees, and have him stand up and pull the pants all the way up.

9. Place pants in front of child. Have him place one foot through one pant leg until his toes show, then place the other foot through the other pant leg, pull them up to his knees, and stand up and pull them all the way up.

As you can see, the nine steps are listed in order from the last step in the procedure, which the child performs first, to the first step, which the child performs last. The reason for this is that *in developing most new desirable behaviors in children, we start with teaching the last step and then work backward* through the step-wise program. We do this because we want the child to have maximum opportunity to practice those steps which always lead to the completion of the target behavior and to reward.

There are five very important points to remember in developing a new behavior in a child.

1. Reward the child with your praise and a bit of his favorite food or other reward each time he successfully completes a step. We want to maximize the child's opportunity for success and the receiving of rewards and minimize his failures. We want the child to learn in a positive way and, thereby, help him build up his self-confidence. Be careful, however, not to reward the child for finishing the same step over and over. The child must also learn that he has to continue to make progress—even if it is slow—if he is to receive a reward.

2. The most basic aspect of the target behavior should be

taught first. Refinements in the target behavior should be taught only after the basic behavior is learned. The successive approximation program (abbreviated: SAP) we have listed for putting on pants, for example, specifically states that the use of buttons, zippers, and similar devices should be avoided.

3. If the child has difficulty mastering a particular step, break up the step into smaller components so that the child can still experience success. Let us suppose that a child exposed to the SAP procedure we have just listed could not pull up his pants from just below his waist. What could we do to make the learning experience a positive one for him? We could break up the step into smaller components. For example, we could place our hands over the child's hands and help him pull up his pants. In this way, he participates in the learning process and his behavior also leads to success and reward. We could then repeat this step until the child learns what to do, and then gradually withdraw our assistance — making sure the child still experiences success.

4. Tell the child what you want him to do before he actually performs the behavior. You eventually want the child to learn to perform the complete target behavior without always having to reward him for doing it. To accomplish this, it is necessary for the child to learn to respond to your instructions. The easiest way for him to learn this is to pair your instructions with his performance of the various steps. Thus, in the SAP procedure for putting on pants, we would first tell the child, "Pull up [put on] your pants," and then encourage him to perform the particular step.

5. Never switch a child who is learning a new desirable behavior from a continuous to an intermittent reward schedule. The performance of steps in a SAP should always be rewarded on a continuous reward basis.

The number of steps in a SAP is largely determined by the child's own capabilities and the therapist's subjective evaluation of how many steps there should be in the program. The general rule is to let the child's behavior guide you in determining how many steps there should be in a SAP and when additional steps should be added.

## WHAT TO CHART

When we are developing a new behavior in a child, it is obviously difficult to chart the number of times the child performs the target behavior. Similarly, we can not record the percentage of correct behaviors. In both cases, the child's charted progress would be zero for a long period of time and not reflect his actual progress.

Instead, we chart the number of steps he has successfully completed in the SAP procedure. To do this, we number the steps in the SAP procedure and then record at the end of each session the last SAP step which the child has completed successfully. If steps are added to the program after treatment begins, the chart as well as the SAP procedure should be renumbered accordingly.

The chart in Figure 7 shows a child's progress through a modified version of the SAP procedure we have presented for putting on pants.

## Behavioral Chaining

After we have developed a number of behaviors in a child (for example, putting on pants, a T-shirt, and socks, and tying shoes), the next step is to teach the child to practice each of these behaviors in sequential order, leading to the final rewarded behavior (for example, dressing himself). The procedure by which we teach a child to perform a sequence of behaviors is *behavioral chaining*.

Behavioral chaining works like a SAP procedure. For example, first we order the behaviors in that sequence which we deem appropriate, as diagramed here for dressing oneself:

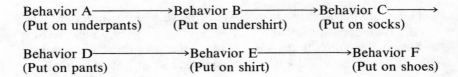

Behavior A————————→Behavior B————————→Behavior C————————→
(Put on underpants)     (Put on undershirt)     (Put on socks)

Behavior D————————→Behavior E————————→Behavior F
(Put on pants)          (Put on shirt)          (Put on shoes)

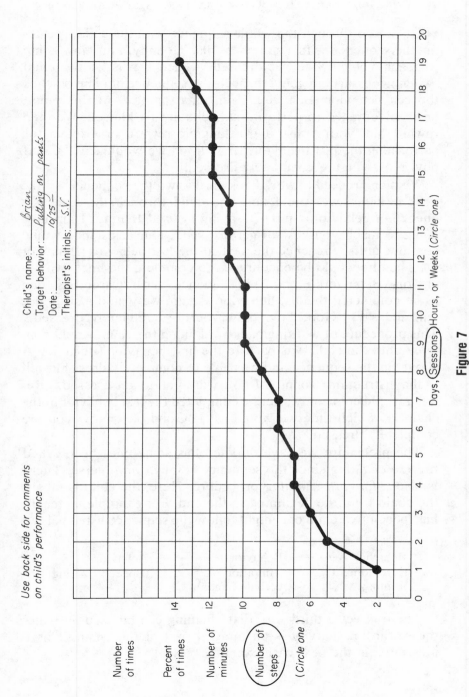

Use back side for comments
on child's performance

Child's name: _Brian_
Target behavior: _Putting on pants_
Date: _10/25_
Therapist's initials: _S.V._

Number
of times

Percent
of times

Number
of minutes

(Number of
steps)

(Circle one)

Days, (Sessions,) Hours, or Weeks (Circle one)

**Figure 7**

CHART SHOWING BRIAN'S PROGRESS IN LEARNING TO PUT ON HIS PANTS BY HIMSELF.

Next, we go through the whole sequence with the child, prefacing the sequence with a statement like "Johnny, I am now going to teach you how to get dressed." Then we assist the child (when necessary) in going through the sequence until he reaches the last behavior (Behavior F in our example). At this point, he is encouraged to perform this behavior by himself. We then reward him with praise and a tangible reward or a token for performing the last behavior. In addition, we would say, "Good boy. Now you are completely dressed."

We then proceed to work backward down the sequence. In the next sessions, we would help the child through the same sequence of behaviors, initially saying again, "Johnny, I am now going to teach you how to get dressed." Our assistance would continue until he reached the next-to-the-last behavior (Behavior E). Then he would be encouraged to complete the next two behaviors (Behaviors E and F) in sequence, and rewarded as soon as he completed the last behavior. Again, we would also praise him and say, "Good boy. Now you are completely dressed." This procedure of working backward along the chain would continue until the child was back to the first behavior (Behavior A above) in the sequence and was able to completely dress himself to the instruction "Johnny, I now want you to get dressed." Reward would come only after he completed the last behavior in the chain, at which time we would say, "Good boy. Now you are completely dressed."

The procedure we have outlined has sometimes been called *reverse chaining* since the sequence is taught in reverse. There is also a *forward chaining* procedure. Here, the child is taught the chain from the beginning to the end. For example, in teaching speech to a child one might follow the sequence listed below:

Behavior A———————→Behavior B———————→Behavior C
(Eye contact                (Imitation of                (Speech training)
training)                     verbal sounds)

There is yet a third way that chaining can be used, in which the rewarding activity is an integral part of the chain. This is illustrated in the next case example.

Marty is a 4½-year-old retarded child who is nonverbal, moderately imitative, and toilet trained. Although he feeds himself now, Marty is still very finicky about what he will eat. His favorite foods are cereal, chocolate pudding, and ice cream. Although he will eat more nutritious foods such as eggs, hamburgers, and juice occasionally, in most cases he will refuse to eat them.

In an attempt to help Marty eat a more balanced diet each day, the following types of chained sequences were arranged for his meals. For breakfast he would have to have one helping of scrambled eggs before he could have the cereal of his choice. Diagramed, this chain is:

Behavior A——————→Behavior B
(Eat eggs)            (Eat cereal)

For lunch, he could not have one of his favorite sandwiches or any ice cream unless he first drank his juice:

Behavior A——————→Behavior B——————————→Behavior C
(Drink juice)       (Eat peanut butter    (Eat ice cream)
                    and jelly sandwich)

Similarly, for dinner he could not have his pudding until he ate his helping of meat:

Behavior A——————→Behavior B
(Eat meat)           (Eat pudding)

Behavioral chaining is an effective way of teaching complex behaviors and behavior sequences. Since reward does not always follow each part of the chain, it is important that the therapy agent praise the child after he completes various sequences in the chain.

## Modeling

One of the most effective procedures for teaching a new behavior to a child involves first demonstrating the behavior yourself and then rewarding the child for successfully trying to imitate what you did. This two-stage procedure is called *modeling* or *imitation learning*, since the child is learning to perform the behavior by imitating what the therapist did.

Modeling often reduces the amount of time a child needs to learn a particular behavior. For example, sometimes a child can learn a SAP procedure much faster if the whole program is first modeled for him by the therapist and then he is rewarded for each successive approximation to what the therapist did. Children can also learn by watching other children perform a target behavior—especially if the child sees that the other children are being rewarded for performing the behavior. The child will soon follow their lead, and he should be rewarded just like the others.

Although modeling is an effective way of teaching children, *the therapist must be sure that the child is very imitative.* Also, the person who performs the modeled behavior should be attractive and/or prestigeful to the child.

## Avoiding Potential Problems And Setbacks

It is often a good idea to anticipate some potential stumbling blocks to effective training and to arrange the training sessions so that such potential difficulties do not occur. Obviously, we cannot anticipate all problems, but many of them can be anticipated and therefore possibly avoided. The following are some difficulties which are often reported by therapy agents.

INTERRUPTIONS DURING THE TRAINING PERIOD

Whenever possible, plan to have your training sessions in a quiet area, during a period of time when you are almost completely confident that you will not be disturbed. Some of the most common interruptions are the telephone, other children who want the therapist's attention, and other adults. The training area should be devoid of objects which are potentially distracting to the child. The area should be well lighted and, when possible, either sound attenuated or away from a noisy street or room. If the room contains a window, make sure the child cannot look outside (better yet, cover it with neutral color drapery or buy a window shade and keep it down). If, on the other hand, it is important for training to take place in the child's "natural" environment, try to anticipate as many potential interruptions as you can and try to prevent them from occurring.

## CHILD SHOWS NEGATIVISM AND/OR REFUSAL TO PARTICIPATE

Sometimes when we begin behavior modification therapy — especially when a new behavior is being developed in a child — the child will show signs of negativism. He may refuse to participate or even throw a tantrum. It is best to handle these situations in a matter-of-fact way. As soon as the child behaves in an undesirable manner, stop treatment and turn away from the child. As soon as he quiets down or stops his negative behavior, turn back toward him and generously reward him with praise for behaving more appropriately. He will soon learn that his negative behavior will not change anything.

If, however, his negativism continues despite your attempts to control it, discontinue training for that session. Review in detail what went on during therapy and during the time period preceding therapy to determine what may have contributed to the child's behavior. Then make any changes which you feel are appropriate. The next session should begin with the same amount of therapist enthusiasm and involvement as before.

## TARGET BEHAVIOR DOES NOT OCCUR OUTSIDE OF THE TRAINING SITUATION

If the target behavior does not seem to generalize to other situations or people, it is best to work with the child in these other situations and also have other people work with him on the same behavior. By doing this, the child will soon learn to generalize the target behavior. To help maintain the child's behavior after training has stopped, be sure to reward the child occasionally for performing the desirable behavior.

BOREDOM OF CHILD OR CHILD'S UNINVOLVEMENT IN THE SAP PROCEDURE

This sometimes means that the therapist is either progressing too slowly, too fast, or is not using a very powerful reward. If the child repeatedly fails particular steps, break down the steps into smaller components until the child can experience success. If the child is progressing through the SAP procedure and shows signs of boredom, the therapist should consider combining various steps in the SAP. You may also want to try different rewards with the child to determine if there is something else for which he would prefer to work.

## Study Questions

1. Choose a child to whom you would like to teach a desirable behavior (perhaps the child you chose on p. 40). Determine whether you want to strengthen a behavior or develop a new behavior. Then develop a treatment using the questions outlined on p. 66.

2. What is *prompting* and why is it used?

(Review pp. 69–70 to check your answer.)

3. Write out a SAP procedure for teaching a child to do one of the following: tie shoes, eat with a spoon, put on a T-shirt. Compare your program with the one listed on pp. 132–134, 121–124, or 127–129.

(Review pp. 73–76 to check your answer.)

4. List the five important points to remember in developing a new behavior in a child.
   a.
   b.
   c.
   d.
   e.

(Review pp. 74–75 to check your answer.)

5. What is *behavioral chaining* and how is it used?

(Review pp. 76–79 to check your answer.)

6. How does behavioral chaining differ from a successive approximation procedure?

(Review pp. 74–78 to check your answer.)

7. How would one use modeling to teach an imitative child to throw a ball?

(Review pp. 79–80 to check your answer.)

# chapter 5

# Reducing
# Undesirable Behaviors
# in Children

*The use of procedures for reducing undesirable behaviors is described in this chapter. We first review the development of a treatment plan. This is followed by a discussion of the use of an extinction procedure, the rewarding of an incompatible desirable behavior, a time out from rewards procedure, a response cost system, a contact desensitization procedure for reducing a child's fear, situational control of a child's behavior, and the use of physical punishment. The chapter ends with a brief discussion of which procedure the therapist should initiate first.*

## Developing A Treatment Plan

We have seen repeatedly that a child's behavior is very much influenced by what happens to him immediately after he performs a particular behavior, and we have learned that when his behavior leads to satisfying or rewarding consequences it will, in most cases, recur the next time the same situation cues are present. Similarly, we find that *when a child's behavior is followed by dissatisfying or unpleasant consequences, his behavior is less likely to recur the next time the same situation cues are present.* This can be diagramed in the following way:

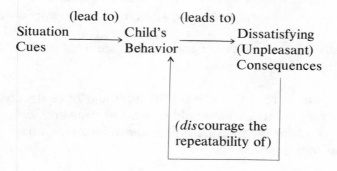

In this chapter, we describe procedures for reducing undesirable behaviors in children. As in any behavior modification procedure, a treatment plan must be formulated *before* treatment is started. Listed here is an outline for developing a treatment plan, which is similar to the one presented in Chapter 4. It should be used by the therapist to help him/her plan out exactly what will happen when the child shows or does not show the undesirable target behavior.

### OUTLINE FOR DEVELOPING A TREATMENT PLAN

1. What is the undesirable target behavior?
2. What method of observation am I going to use?
3. What am I going to chart?
   a. Circle one:
      Number of times
      Percent of times
      Number of minutes
      Number of steps
   b. Circle one:
      Sessions
      Days
      Hours
      Weeks
4. How long will the baseline period be?
5. What is my criterion of success?
6. What will I do *specifically* when my child (the child I am working with) makes an undesirable response?
7. What will I do *specifically* when my child makes a desirable response?
8. Any additional comments about the treatment procedure?

After you have read through this chapter and have decided on a treatment approach, you should be able to answer each of these questions. Once the treatment plan is established, you are ready to begin treatment.

## The Use of Extinction

Children tend to perform certain undesirable behaviors because they are (or have been) rewarded for performing them. Thus, just as it is possible to strengthen a desirable behavior by rewarding the child each time the behavior occurs, it is also possible to reduce an undesirable behavior by making certain that you do not reward the child when he performs the behavior. *Extinction refers to the removal of those rewarding consequences which normally follow a particular behavior.*

In order to use this procedure, the therapist *must* be able to identify those consequences which are rewarding the child's undesirable behavior and be in a position in which he/she can determine whether or not those consequences will follow the child's behavior.

To understand what could possibly be rewarding the child's behavior, the therapist should apply the procedure discussed in Chapter 2 for the identification of situation cues and consequences. For example, he should ask the following questions: "What happens immediately before the undesirable behavior occurs?" "What happens immediately after the behavior occurs?" One of the most common reward consequences for a child's undesirable behavior is the adult (or peer) attention which he receives.

After you determine what is rewarding the target behavior, make sure that the child does not receive this reward when he performs the behavior. Do not expect his behavior to decrease immediately—in fact, *you should first expect an increase in the occurrence of the undesirable behavior before you begin to notice a decrease.* Each of us knows this to be true from his or her own life. For example, if I walk into my study at night and turn the light switch to *On* but do not receive a reward by having the light go on, my first reaction is to flip the switch from *On* to *Off* to *On* to *Off* to *On* repeatedly until I am sure the light will not go on. Then I stop flipping the switch (behavior is on extinction) and go and find a new light bulb—or call an electrician. Here my reaction—as is the case with children—was to first increase the occurrence of the flipping-the-switch behavior and then decrease it because reward did not follow. The following case example illustrates the use of extinction with a 3½-year-old schizophrenic child named Phil.

> Phil has recently begun to cry loudly and scream whenever
> his mother puts him to sleep at his regular bedtime. His

mother paid little attention to his crying, believing that he would stop eventually. During the first few evenings, she was right. He stopped crying and screaming after about 15 minutes, and then she looked in on him to make sure he was all right.

Toward the end of the week, however, he did not stop crying after 15 minutes, so she decided to enter his room to make sure he was safe. He stopped crying as soon as she opened the door, and began crying again after she closed the door. Twenty minutes later he was still crying, so she went back into his room, picked him up, and tried to comfort him for a few minutes.

As soon as Phil quieted down, she placed him back in his bed and left the room. He began crying again — finally going to sleep 2 ½ hours later. This pattern of crying followed by mother's intervention continued for five more days until the mother sought help from her pediatrician who, in turn, referred her to a university clinic.

The psychologist at the clinic sent an observer into the home to objectively determine what happened between mother and child at the child's bedtime. The mother and father were asked to "do what you normally do" for the next three nights and not change the normal routine. The mother was also asked to record how many minutes it took Phil to fall asleep (or stop crying for 45 consecutive minutes) after putting him to bed. Over the three-night period, Phil fell asleep (or stopped crying for 45 minutes) after an average of 165 minutes.

For the fourth night, Mrs. Barker was told to resist any temptation to enter Phil's room while he was crying unless she was sure he had injured himself. She was also told to remove any toys or objects from his room which could possibly injure him if he became very angry at night. Mrs. Barker followed these instructions, although very hesitantly.

The first night Phil cried and screamed for almost five hours — stopping, at times, for about 10 to 15 minutes — before he finally fell asleep. When she was sure he was asleep, she went into his room and was glad to see everything was all right. The second night Phil cried for three hours, and by the eighth night he cried for only 15 minutes. Within two weeks, he no longer cried or screamed before going to sleep. A chart of Phil's progress appears in Figure 8.

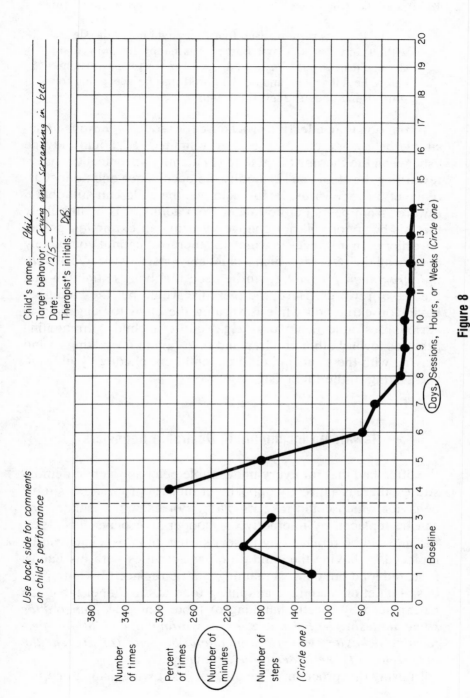

**Figure 8**

CHART SHOWING THE REDUCTION IN PHIL'S CRYING IN BED USING AN EXTINCTION PROCEDURE.

The Barkers were pleased that Phil could now fall asleep without any "fuss." Mrs. Barker was happy to know that she could now put him to bed, spend more time with him before he fell asleep, and not be afraid that he was going to start crying once she left the room.

Extinction is an effective procedure for reducing various undesirable behaviors, but its use is very limited. It should only be used when the therapist is able to (1) identify specifically what is rewarding the child and (2) modify the occurrence and nonoccurrence of these rewards. If, for example, the child can still obtain rewards from peers but no longer from adults, it is highly likely that his behavior will not change by using an extinction procedure alone. In instances in which the therapist cannot completely control all the rewards which a child may possibly receive, a *multiple treatment procedure* can be used involving extinction and the use of rewards. Here, the therapist would put the target behavior on extinction while rewarding the child for engaging in various desirable behaviors — e.g., ignore a child's threatening gestures toward other children and reward him for talking to and playing with the same and different children, playing by himself, and talking to the therapist.

## Rewarding Incompatible Desirable Behaviors

We often find that for every undesirable behavior a child demonstrates, there is a directly opposite or more appropriate desirable behavior which could take its place. For example, isolate play can be replaced by interactive or cooperative play, out-of-seat running can be replaced by in-seat sitting, thumbsucking can be replaced by having the child do other activities with his hands, repeated loud bursts of screaming can be replaced by long periods of quiet or reading, and spilling food at the dinner table can be replaced by careful handling of food. Thus, *we can reduce some undesirable behaviors by rewarding the child for performing behaviors which are incompatible with (or prevent the occurrence of) the undesirable behaviors.*

In using this procedure, we are not just extinguishing one undesirable behavior and rewarding another desirable behavior; rather, we are teaching the child to perform a behavior which is incompatible with his performance of the undesirable behavior. A child can not mumble and talk clearly at the same time, run around in the classroom and sit in his seat at the same time, slap his face with both hands and hold a teddy bear with both hands at the same time, and so forth. The successful use of this procedure, therefore, depends on (1) how adept the therapist is in identifying a behavior which is incompatible with the undesirable behavior and (2) whether the therapist can find a reward which is powerful (and attractive) enough to outweigh the positive factors associated with the child's performance of the undesirable behavior. Obviously, as the desirable behavior increases in occurrence, the undesirable behavior will occur less frequently.

The following case example involving a verbal, hyperactive, five-year-old child who showed signs of minimal brain damage illustrates the use of this procedure.

> Bill was brought to the clinic by his parents, who reported that for the last six months he had been "virtually uncontrollable" in the home. He climbed on furniture and on guests who came into the home, did not sit still at the dinner table, spilled food, "constantly" ran in and out the back door, and did not fall asleep until late in the evening.
>
> Mr. and Mrs. Thomas were asked to choose one particular situation which was especially annoying to them and which they would like to deal with first. They chose Bill's behavior at mealtime. Specifically, the target behavior was sitting at the dinner table kicking the legs of the chair or moving from side to side in the chair.
>
> The Thomases were asked to observe Bill for five days at each dinner meal and to record separately with a stopwatch the number of minutes he spent performing the target behavior. They discovered that on the average he spent about 15 minutes moving around in his chair and kicking it during a 20-minute meal.
>
> They were next asked to choose a reward which was very attractive to Bill and to give bits of this reward to him after he sat quietly for 20 seconds (sitting quietly is incompatible with kicking the chair legs and moving around in the chair). This was to occur for the next three days.

The Thomases returned on the fourth day and reported that Bill's undesirable behavior had begun to decrease — although he was still moving around for, on the average, about 12 minutes. They were then instructed to continue the procedure for another four meals. Upon their return, they said that he was now down to about 8 minutes per meal. They were then told to vary the use of his favorite rewards (various sweet desserts) and to increase the sitting quiet time interval to 40 seconds for the next seven days.

Bill seemed to adjust easily to this new schedule and the different rewards. Within five days he was sitting quietly at the dinner table for 15 minutes, and by the end of the week he was quiet for almost 17 minutes. His behavior at the table continued to improve, and at the end of three and a half weeks he was sitting still for practically the whole meal (19 minutes). His parents had also begun to withdraw gradually the use of his favorite desserts and, instead, to praise him for behaving so quietly.

As you can see from this example, the most favorable aspect of the procedure (especially when you compare it to some of the other procedures described in this chapter) is that the therapist is strengthening a desirable (adaptive) behavior as he/she is reducing an undesirable behavior.

## Time Out From Rewards

A very effective way of reducing a child's undesirable behavior involves removing him/her from an attractive and rewarding situation (or withdrawing a rewarding activity or event from him) for a certain time period *immediately following* his performance of the target behavior. This procedure is called *time out from rewards,* or just "time out." Each time the child shows the undesirable behavior, we take him out of the rewarding situation and place him in a situation where, presumably, his undesirable behavior will not be rewarded.

The type of situation in which the child is placed is very important. If, for example, the child performs the target behavior and you send him to his room, you may think that this is sufficient.

But if the child's room contains many interesting toys, a television which he can watch at any time, books and magazines, a radio or record player that he can listen to, and so forth, the probability that removal to this room will have any effect on his undesirable behavior is quite small. The situation or area to which the child is sent should be, whenever possible, devoid of interesting and distracting objects (as well as objects potentially dangerous to him) and should be far enough away from the rewarding situation so that the child can not hear what is going on. *The "time out area," therefore, must have many fewer positive aspects associated with it than the rewarding area.* If a time out area is not readily available, you can place the child in a chair (facing the wall) in a remote corner or section of a classroom, living room, kitchen, dormitory room, dayroom, and so forth. Or, you can construct or purchase a "portable" time out room such as the one described in Appendix F.

The child should be allowed to return to the rewarding situation as soon as the undesirable behavior has stopped or within a few minutes (usually three to five minutes). The child should not be permitted to stay in the time out area for an extended period of time. When the child is brought to the time out area, the therapist should carry out this activity matter-of-factly with as little verbal and emotional interaction as possible. Similarly, while the child is brought back to the rewarding situation, the therapist should make every effort to interact with him only in a matter-of-fact fashion. Then, when they are back in the rewarding situation, the therapist should respond to the child in his/her normal way. Whenever possible, the therapist should reward the child for behaving in a desirable way when he is in the rewarding situation. *Children learn to reduce their undesirable behavior more readily when they observe that satisfying consequences follow some of their behaviors and dissatisfying consequences follow other behaviors.*

The following case example illustrates the use of time out.

Beth is an eight-year-old moderately retarded girl who is verbal, interactive, and overweight. She enjoys her special education classes and looks forward to going to school each day. One of Beth's main problems in school is that she hits other children and occasionally pinches them. Her teacher had tried in vain to change Beth's behavior. She then decided to use a time out procedure.

The teacher observed Beth for a five-day baseline period and counted the number of times she hit or pinched another child. The teacher then told Beth that she would lose the privilege of staying in the classroom whenever she hit or pinched another child. Within 10 minutes, Beth hit another child while they were painting. The teacher went to Beth, told her, "You do not hit people!" took her hand, and brought her outside the classroom and into an adjacent small vacant room which had only two chairs in it. Beth started crying just as her teacher left the room.

Five minutes later, the teacher returned to the room and said, "You can come out now," and accompanied Beth back to the classroom. This procedure was continued over a five-week period until Beth's undesirable behavior was no longer a problem. During this five-week period, the teacher also tried to praise Beth whenever she saw her playing with other children and not hitting or pinching them.

Another time out procedure, called *withdrawal of rewards,* does not require the therapist to remove the child physically from the rewarding situation. Instead, *the therapist has to remove what is rewarding to the child.* For example, if a child hits his face in a self-injurious manner and also enjoys physical stimulation and contact by the therapist, the therapist could use the withdrawal of his/her stimulation and contact each time the child hit himself. The withdrawal of such contact, as well as its presence during periods without hitting, will help the child learn which behavior will produce dissatisfying consequences and which behaviors will lead to continued satisfying consequences.

The rewarding situation should be returned to the child when the target behavior (e.g., self-injurious behavior, tantrum, screaming) stops, or within a three- to five-minute period. Moreover, the reward should be returned in the same matter-of-fact manner in which it was withdrawn. Once the reward is back, however, the therapist should again respond to the child in his/her normal way and praise the child for continuing to perform desirable alternative behaviors.

It is important to remember that time out should (1) only be used in an environment or situation which the child finds very rewarding, (2) be administered in a matter-of-fact way immediately following the occurrence of the undesirable behavior, and (3) not be used indiscriminately by the therapist for any undesirable behavior—only for the target behavior.

## Response Cost

Many therapists find that once a token economy system is established with a child or group of children (e.g., a special education classroom), a procedure is "built into" the system for reducing undesirable behaviors. Specifically, some therapists discover that placing a price on undesirable behavior(s) results in the reduction of that behavior.

> Sharon is a 10-year-old, verbal, borderline retarded girl who attends and enjoys public school classes. Although she is quite well behaved at school, her parents report that she is a "behavior problem" at home. Their success with stopping her hitting of her younger brother and her negativism ("No!" "I won't do that!") has been minimal.
>
> After consulting a psychologist, they initiated a token economy system in the home for Sharon for about one month (they decided not to include Bobby, their younger son, since they felt he was too young for such a program). Sharon received tokens for various activities and exchanged tokens for various "rewards and things." After about one month, Sharon was also charged tokens each time she hit Bobby (10 tokens) and each time she talked back to her parents in a negative way (1–5 tokens, depending on the severity of her negativism).
>
> Sharon liked "being paid" for doing various activities around the house and being able to exchange the tokens for different foods and other items. She did object, however, to being charged for "doing bad things," although she admitted that she would not like these "things" done to her. The token system was arranged so that the extent of Sharon's undesirable behavior during the day was reflected in how many tokens she had left at the end of the day. On those days that Sharon behaved especially badly, she would

not have any tokens left at the end of the day; on those days that she showed a few undesirable behaviors, she would end up the day with a few tokens to spend; and, on those days when she was especially well behaved, she had many tokens to spend.

Sharon's undesirable behavior decreased to a minimal level within five weeks, although there were still occasional outbursts toward her parents. Her parents decided to keep the system going in the house and modify it as her undesirable behavior decreased even more.

A response cost procedure is obviously not for every child who is on a token system. The child should be verbal and capable of understanding *why* certain behaviors lead to the receipt of tokens and other behaviors lead to the taking away of tokens. The therapist must also make sure that the child has sufficient opportunity to receive tokens throughout the day for activities which vary in the amount they pay. The system should not be a negative or deficit spending system, and the therapist should not use it indiscriminatively. The child should be able to earn enough tokens each day to offset the number which have been charged to him for performing the target behavior. If this does not occur the system should be changed. Finally, this procedure should not be instituted until the normal token system is well established, and the therapist should make sure that the child does not regard the whole token system as unpleasant — whether he receives tokens for desirable behavior or has tokens taken away.

## Contact Desensitization For Fears

Fear is a very strong emotion and is associated with many signs of anxiety — for example, rapid pulse rate, tense muscles, irritability, and "butterflies" in the stomach. When a child experiences fear in a situation where there is no obvious danger, his/her fear is irrational. When the child begins to avoid the nondangerous feared situation, his fear then becomes a *fear reaction* (or phobic reaction).

Fear reactions are very common in children. Some are so common (e.g., fear of dogs and other animals, the dark, ghosts, bugs) that we often view them as "normal." Some fear reactions are fleeting, while others persist over time. When a child's fear becomes intolerable, however, or prevents him from carrying out normal, everyday activities or visiting nondangerous places, then the treatment of his fear becomes necessary.

One of the most successful procedures for reducing fears in children is called *contact desensitization*. In this procedure, the therapist, through his/her contact with the child, carries out a series of steps to help the child become *desensitized* to the feared object or situation.

The desensitization process is accomplished by gradually exposing the child in small steps to the feared object or situation *after* each step has been modeled first by the therapist. After modeling a step, the therapist helps the child perform that step— touching the child to help guide him, encouraging the child with various motivating statements, and praising the child for making progress. What is also important in the desensitization process is the type of relationship that exists between the therapist and the child. The therapist should make sure that he/she has established a good, positive relationship with the child, and conveys warmth toward the child, before initiating this procedure.

The desensitization procedure consists of three major components: (1) identification of the target behavior, (2) construction of a graduated hierarchy of steps toward the feared object or situation, and (3) treatment proper.

As is the case with any behavior being modified, the target behavior should be specifically identified by the therapy agent. In the case of a child's fear, it is important for the therapist to identify not only what the child is afraid of, but also the situation(s) in which the fear reaction occurs. Next, the therapist should develop the graduated hierarchy. It should be constructed with a great deal of care, and should start with the least fearful step that the child can perform (without any trouble) and proceed down to the most fearful step. Here is an example of a hierarchy used with children who were afraid to go into a swimming pool:[3]

---

[3]Based on a study by Morris, R. J., & Morisano, E. The treatment of aquaphobia in retarded persons via contact desensitization. Unpublished study. Syracuse University, 1974.

1. Let's begin by walking into the pool room to the white marker (one-quarter of the way to the pool).
2. Walk to the yellow marker on the floor (half of the way).
3. Walk to the red marker on the floor (three-quarters of the way).
4. Walk to the green marker by the edge of the pool.
5. Sit down right there (by the edge of the pool).
6. Let's see you put your feet in the water, while I slowly count to 9.   1. . .2. . .3
7. . . .4. . .5. . .6
8. . . .7. . .8. . .9
9. Get up and walk into the water to the red marker and stay there until I count to 6.   1. . .2. . .3
10. . . .4. . .5. . .6
11. Walk to the green marker (halfway down ramp) and stay there until I count to 6.   1. . .2. . .3
12. . . .4. . .5. . .6
13. Walk to the yellow marker (bottom of ramp: 2'6" deep) and stay there until I count to 9. You can hold onto the edge.   1. . .2. . .3
14. . . .4. . .5. . .6
15. . . .7. . .8. . .9
16. Let's see if you can stand there without holding on (only if person held on in previous step).
17. Walk out to the red marker (3' from edge) and then come back to me.
18. Splash some water on yourself; hold on to the edge if you like.
19. Do that without holding on (only if person held on in previous step).
20. Splash some water on your face; you may hold on to the edge if you like.
21. Do that without holding on (only if person held on in previous step).
22. Squat down and blow some bubbles in the water. You can hold on if you like.
23. Blow bubbles without holding on (only if person held on in previous step).

24. Put your whole face in the water. You may hold on if you like.
25. Do that again without holding on (only if person held on in previous step).
26. Put your whole body under water. You can hold on if you like.
27. Do that again without holding on (only if person held on in previous step).
28. Walk out into the water up to your chin (if pool depth permits).
29. Hold onto this kickboard and put your face in the water.
30. Hold onto the kickboard and take one foot off the ground.
31. Hold onto the kickboard and take both feet off the ground.
32. Put your face in the water again and take your feet off the bottom.
33. Let's go down to the deep end of the pool. Sit on the edge and put your feet in the water.
34. O.K. Now climb down the ladder.
35. Now hold onto the edge right here by the green marker.
36. While still holding on, put your whole body under water.
37. Hold onto the kickboard.
38. While still holding on put your face in the water.
39. Do that again, but now put your whole head under water.
40. O.K. Now climb out of the pool and come over to the blue marker. Jump in the water right here (at pool depth of 3'6" or 5' depending on person's height).

Most hierarchies contain 20 to 30 items. It is not unusual, however, for those hierarchies that represent a narrowly focused fear to have fewer items and those hierarchies that represent a complex fear to contain more items. Regardless of the number of items, the final hierarchy should represent a slow and smooth gradation of steps.

Following the formation of the hierarchy, the therapist initiates the actual treatment. The therapist models the first step on the hierarchy and then encourages the child to imitate the therapist. The child is physically guided by the therapist, encouraged, and praised for his progress. This procedure is continued for each step on the hierarchy. After the child develops confidence in performing some of the early steps (after he has practiced them many times with the therapist's assistance), the therapist can gradually withdraw his modeling and guidance, although he should continue praising and encouraging the child. The therapist should continue the modeling, guiding, encouraging, and praising on the later steps. A prescriptive program describing this procedure is presented in Chapter 6 (pp. 157–159).

## Situation Control

In many instances, a therapy agent is not interested in reducing or eliminating a child's behavior; rather, he/she wants to teach the child to perform the behavior *only* in certain situations. This is called *situation* (or *stimulus*) *control.* In some situations the behavior is desirable; in others it is undesirable. *The goal of therapy is to restrict the child's behavior to those situations in which it is desirable.*

For example, instead of permitting a child to either urinate or have a bowel movement in his pants, we would prefer to teach him where and under what circumstances he should perform these behaviors. Specifically, we would want him to be sitting on (or standing in front of) a toilet with his pants down before he performed either activity. We would not want a child to take off his clothes in the middle of a downtown street; rather, we would want to teach him, for example, to remove his pants in those situations in which his mother says, "Get undressed and get ready for bed." Similarly, it is appropriate for a child to run and jump outside in the schoolyard during playtime, but it is not desirable for that child to run and jump in the classroom during storytime or the reading period.

To assist the child in learning where and when he can and cannot perform the behavior, we have to help him *discriminate* between permissible situations (PER) and nonpermissible situations (not-PER). The best way to teach him is to first make sure that PER and not-PER are obviously different. For example, whenever possible the immediate surroundings of PER should be different from not-PER. The color of the walls and floor in PER should be different from not-PER, the types of activities that usually go on in PER should be different, and the instructions from the therapist (or therapy assistants) preceding PER should differ from not-PER. Finally, if the time of day for PER can be arranged so that it differs from not-PER, this would also be advisable.

Next, the therapist should reward the child for performing the behavior in PER and never reward him for performing the behavior in not-PER. The therapist should also make sure that the child does not receive reward from other sources in not-PER. Alternately, the therapist may want to use one of the other procedures discussed in this chapter during this period. For example, the therapist could use a time out procedure, a response cost program if the child is on a token economy system, or reward a behavior which is incompatible with the undesirable behavior. *Whichever method is used in not-PER, the therapist should continue rewarding the child in PER.*

Before situation control is taught to a child, the therapist should be sure that the child (1) is able to pay attention to the therapist, (2) can at least minimally attend to situational differences, and (3) is able to follow simple commands (e.g., "Come to me"; "Sit down!"). If the child cannot perform all three of these activities, he should be taught them first. As the child learns to discriminate successfully when and where to perform the target behavior, the therapist — if it seems necessary — can begin gradually to lessen the distinct differences between PER and not-PER. The differences, however, should never be made so small that the child again has trouble discriminating between the two types of situations.

## The Use of Physical Punishment

The next procedure is the least preferred by the author and the least recommended. It involves the use of physical punishment. The use of such punishment very often results in unpleasant or unwanted side effects. Some potential side effects are the following:

1. Punishment often suppresses a child's undesirable behavior but does not change it. Once a child realizes or observes that physical punishment will no longer follow the undesirable behavior, the behavior is likely to recur.

2. Although punishment may reduce or eliminate a particular behavior, other undesirable behaviors may develop.

3. Punishment often produces emotional responses in the child such as unnecessary anxiety and fear responses.

4. The therapist who administers the punishment may become the recipient of aggression and hostility from the child. This side effect would also influence the nature of the therapist-child relationship — possibly leading the child to become fearful of and also avoid the therapist.

5. A generalization gradient may develop, whereby the child not only avoids performing the undesirable behavior but also avoids participating in various activities in the punishment situation (or he may avoid entering the situation completely).

6. Punishment may have no effect on the child's undesirable behavior, or it may even lead to an increase in the behavior — especially where the child views the attention he receives from the therapist as a *reward* for the undesirable behavior.

In some rare instances, however, physical punishment (e.g., a painful event like a slap or a loud noise) must be used. Before the therapist carries out this procedure, he/she should consider the following questions:

1. What are the risks involved for the child, for myself, for the institution, school, or hospital for which I work? (If the procedure is used, the therapist should make sure that he/she has the parents' written consent for the use of this procedure and that the institution's, school's, or hospital's administration has approved the use of the procedure.)

2. Have all other possible procedures been shown to have no or little effect on the child's behavior?

3. Do the potential positive effects of using the procedure outweigh the possible negative side effects?

4. Is the child's behavior so undesirable that it needs to be changed?

Once these questions are answered, and the decision has been made to use the procedure, the therapist should apply the physical punishment in a consistent fashion and *immediately* following the occurrence of the undesirable behavior. The therapist should also make sure that he/she rewards the child throughout the day for performing various desirable behaviors as well as those behavior(s) which are incompatible with the undesirable behavior. It is also helpful to pair a preliminary cue (e.g., a neutral mechanical sound, or the verbalization "No") with the punishment. In this way, the therapist may be able to use the cue once in a while instead of the physical punishment to reduce the behavior.

## Which Procedure To Use?

After reading about each of the procedures described in this chapter, the question which arises for a therapist is, "Which procedure should I use?" The question is not an easy one to answer, but certain guidelines can be provided. *Whenever possible, a therapist should first use the incompatible behavior procedure.* This is clearly the most preferred procedure. Instead of this method, the therapist could initiate an extinction procedure, but this is not recommended when there is an obvious incompatible behavior available which can be taught to the child. If neither of these procedures is effective in reducing the child's behavior, and a token economy system has been established, then the therapist should use the response cost procedure. A time out procedure could also be initiated. Physical punishment should be used only after all previous procedures have been used unsuccessfully, and only after the various questions listed previously have been carefully considered. Most important, however, no matter what procedure is chosen, is that the therapist make sure that he/she (and the therapy assistants or colleagues) is *consistent* in the application of each procedure.

## Study Questions

1. Choose a child whose undesirable behavior you would like to reduce. Based on the material presented in this chapter, formulate a treatment plan using the outline listed on p. 88.

2. What are the two major limitations associated with the use of an extinction procedure?

(Review p. 92 to check your answer.)

3. What should you first expect to happen to a child's undesirable behavior when you begin an extinction procedure?

(Review p. 89 to check your answer.)

4. List five undesirable childhood behaviors and their corresponding incompatible desirable behaviors.

| *Undesirable Behavior* | *Incompatible Behavior* |
|---|---|
| a. | |
| b. | |
| c. | |
| d. | |
| e. | |

5. What two factors largely determine the success of a treatment program involving the use of an incompatible behavior modification procedure?
   a.
   b.
   (Review p. 93 to check your answer.)

6. Why is the type of situation in which the child is placed important in a time out procedure?

(Review pp. 94–95 to check your answer.)

7. What are the two ways in which time out can be used?
   a.
   b.

(Review pp. 94–96 to check your answer.)

8. A response cost procedure should only be used when a _____ is in existence.

(Review p. 97 to check your answer.)

9. What are the three major components of contact desensitization?
   a.
   b.
   c.

(Review p. 99 to check your answer.)

10. Contact desensitization consists of therapist touch, encouragement, praise, and _____ .

(Review p. 99 to check your answer.)

11. When should a therapist use the situation control procedure?

(Review p. 102 to check your answer.)

12. Why should the PER differ from the not-PER?

(Review pp. 102–103 to check your answer.)

13. List four potential side effects of the use of physical punishment.
    a.
    b.

c.

d.

(Review p. 104 to check your answer.)

14. What procedure should be combined with the use of punishment?

(Review p. 105 to check your answer.)

15. No matter which procedure a therapist uses, he/she should make sure that he is _____ .

(Review p. 105 to check your answer.)

# chapter 6

# Prescriptions For Treating Particular Target Behaviors

*In this chapter, we present a series of behavioral prescriptions for teaching various target behaviors to children. These prescriptions are presented in a step-wise fashion and are intended to aid the therapist in developing expertise in treating various children's behaviors. Prescriptions are included for various social and self-help skills.*

## Use of The Behavioral Prescriptions

The behavioral prescriptions presented in this chapter are designed for those children who do not show (or demonstrate only minimally) the target behavior being taught. For those children who can perform some (but not all) of the steps listed in a particular behavioral prescription, the therapist may have to change the program to adapt it to the particular child. Changes in a prescription may also be necessary for other reasons. The therapist, however, should arrange any revised prescriptive program so that it (1) proceeds in gradual steps and (2) gives the therapist the opportunity to guide the child through some of the difficult steps before the child is requested to perform those steps by himself.

Throughout the use of each prescriptive program, the therapist should praise the child for any progress and reward him with small amounts of his favorite food, drink, or other reward. If tokens are used as rewards, make sure that the child is thoroughly familiar with the tokens and *what* can be "purchased" with the tokens after the session is over. You should also chart the child's progress, circling the appropriate phrase on the vertical line of the chart (e.g., "Percent of Times" or "Number of Steps") and circling "Sessions" on the horizontal line of the chart. Be sure to keep a record of the child's progress during each session so that you can readily transfer this information to his chart at the end of the session.

Before applying a program, the therapist should read through the program in its entirety and make sure that he thoroughly understands the steps as well as the comments made at the end.[4]

---

[4]Many of the programs presented in this chapter were developed during the conduct of research and the development of demonstration projects at the Syracuse Developmental Center, Syracuse, New York.

## PROGRAM FOR EYE CONTACT TRAINING[5]

The therapist should work with each child on an individual basis at least once per day, 5 to 10 minutes per session.

### TRAINING SETTING

Eye contact training should take place in a quiet room, devoid of any distractions. Ideally, the room should contain two chairs and a table. It should be well lighted, sound attenuated, and not very large. The two chairs should face each other and the table should be placed to the side of the therapist's chair. The table will be used to record correct and incorrect responses on the tally sheet and to keep the child's rewards out of his/her reach. The child's chair should be small enough to enable his feet to touch the floor.

### EQUIPMENT AND MATERIALS NEEDED

1. A stopwatch or a large clock with an easily observable second hand. The stopwatch or clock should be placed outside the child's reach and clearly in view of the therapist — if possible, the large clock should be hung on the wall behind the child.
2. Two wrist (golf) counters of different colors or a tally sheet and pencil.
3. A graph to chart the child's progress. The vertical line should state "Percent of Correct Eye Contacts," and the horizontal line should state "Sessions."

### PROCEDURE

A. *Baseline Level.* Before training begins, you should conduct

---

[5]This prescription is based on a study by Morris, R. J., & O'Neill, J. H. Developing eye contact in severely and profoundly retarded children. *Mental Retardation*, 1975, *13*, 42–43.

five baseline observation sessions. Bring the child to the room and sit him/her down opposite you.

1. Say the command, "[Name], look at me."
2. If the child makes direct eye contact with you within a 10-second period, *say nothing and do not give him/her anything as a reward.* Just record a correct response on the tally sheet by placing a plus sign on the sheet or by pressing one of the wrist counters one time.
3. If the child does not make direct eye contact with you within the 10-second period, *say nothing and do not give him anything as a reward.* Just record an incorrect response on the tally sheet by placing a minus sign on the sheet or by pressing the other wrist counter one time.
4. After 10 seconds have elapsed, say the command again. Continue this 10-second sequence until the designated 5- to 10-minute treatment time has ended.
5. Be sure to add up the number of correct (+) and incorrect (−) responses for each session. After the session is over, *calculate and then record the percent of correct eye contacts* on the child's chart and compare his/her performance with the previous sessions.

B. *Treatment Phase.* This phase is conducted in essentially the same way as the baseline phase except we reward the child for correct responses (with social praise for correct responses as well as small amounts of the child's favorite food, candy, or drink).

1. Before each treatment period begins, determine which type of reward the child would prefer. Offer the child three or four of his favorite types of food and see which one he seems to like best at that time. This should be the reward that you start using for that particular session. If the child seems to become bored with that reward, or unresponsive, switch to his next preferred item.
2. If the child makes direct eye contact to the command "[Name], look at me," then say, "Very good (or "Good boy"/"Good girl") . . . I am so happy," and give him/her a bit of the favorite food or drink. Then record a correct response on your tally sheet (plus sign) or wrist counter.
3. If the child does not make direct eye contact in response

to your command "[Name], look at me," then *say nothing and do not give him/her anything as a reward.* Record an incorrect response on your tally sheet (minus sign) or other wrist counter.

4. This sequence of giving the child a reward or nothing each time he looks at you, as well as recording his correct and incorrect responses, should be continued until the 5- to 10-minute treatment time has ended.

5. After the session, add up the number of correct and incorrect responses. Then *calculate and record the percent of correct eye contacts* on the child's chart and compare his/her progress with the previous sessions.

6. The treatment phase should continue until the child reaches at least 90 percent or above correct eye contacts per session for three consecutive sessions.

If the child does not respond at all initially to your instruction to "Look at me," you should use a *prompting procedure.* Prompting helps the child learn what the desirable behavior is. First, you should give your instruction, "[Name], look at me." Then, you should gently grasp his head with your hands and slowly turn it so that he is looking at your eyes. Reward and praise him when he looks at you. The next time, he should be given the opportunity to look at you without prompting. If he does not look at you, again say "[Name], look at me," and gently move his head until his eyes meet yours. Prompting is continued until the child learns what behavior he is supposed to perform in the particular situation. It is important, however, to be sure that you lessen your assistance as the child makes progress toward performing the correct behavior. After awhile you will notice that he will make the desired response without your assistance — although it may take a number of sessions.

## PROGRAM FOR IMITATION LEARNING[6]

Each child should be worked with on an individual basis at least once per day, 10 minutes per session.

### TRAINING SETTING

Imitation training should take place in a quiet room, devoid of any distractions. Ideally, the room should not contain any furniture except two chairs and a small table. The two chairs should face each other and the table should be placed to the side of the therapist's chair. The table will be used to record correct and incorrect responses on the tally sheet and to keep the child's rewards out of his/her reach. The room should be well lighted, sound attenuated, and not very large. The child's chair should be small enough to enable his/her feet to touch the floor.

### EQUIPMENT AND MATERIALS NEEDED

1. A stopwatch or a large clock with an easily observable second hand. The stopwatch or clock should be placed outside the child's reach and clearly in view of the therapist—if possible, the large clock should be hung on the wall behind the child.
2. Two wrist (golf) counters of different colors or a tally sheet and pencil.
3. A graph to chart the child's progress. The vertical line should state "Percent of Correct Imitations" and the horizontal line should state "Sessions."

---

[6]This program is based on a study by Baer, D. M., Peterson, R. F., & Sherman, J. A. The development of imitation by reinforcing behavioral similarity to a model. *Journal of Experimental Analysis of Behavior,* 1967, *10,* 405–416; and a study by O'Neill, J. H., and Morris, R. J. The development of imitation in nonimitative profoundly retarded children: Contribution of reinforcement and instructions. Unpublished study. Syracuse University, 1974.

PROCEDURE

A. *Baseline.* Following eye contact training (three successive sessions with 90 percent or greater eye contact response), the child should be brought to the same room and seated opposite the therapist.
   1. Say the command, "[Name], do this!" At the same time, the first of the 15 responses presented here should be modeled by the therapist:

      Raise both arms
      Place hands on chest
      Place hands on knees
      Touch nose with one hand
      Touch stomach with both hands
      Touch ears with both hands
      Place hands over eyes
      Place both hands on top of head
      Stretch both hands to the sides
      Protrude tongue
      Clap hands
      Touch elbow with hand
      Nod head
      Tap chair
      Stamp feet

   2. This response should be performed until the child imitates your response, or for a maximum period of 10 seconds.
   3. If the child imitates you, *say nothing and do not reward him/her,* but record his success on one of the wrist counters or on the tally sheet.
   4. If the child does not imitate, say nothing and do not reward, and record an incorrect response on the tabulation sheet or on the other wrist counter.
   5. After 10 seconds has elapsed, you should perform the next response. If the child imitates you correctly,

you should record a correct response. If he does not imitate you, record an incorrect response.

6. Continue saying one command every 10 seconds until the end of the 10-minute session.
7. Be sure to add up the number of correct and incorrect responses for each session. After each session, calculate and then record the *percent of correct imitations* for that session on the graph.

B. *Treatment.* This phase is essentially the same as baseline; however, correct responses are rewarded with small amounts of food or liquids and social praise ("Very good! Good boy[girl]!").

1. Before each treatment period begins, determine which type of reward the child prefers. Offer the child three or four of his favorite types of food or drink and see which one he seems to like best at that time. This should be the reward that you start using for that particular session. If the child seems to become bored with that reward, or unresponsive, switch to his next preferred item.
2. If the child makes a correct imitative response to the command "[Name], do this," then say "Very Good! Good boy[girl]!" and give him/her a bit of the favorite food or drink. Then record his correct response.
3. If the child gives an incorrect or no response, say nothing and do not give him anything as a reward.
4. This sequence of giving the child a reward or nothing each time he has the opportunity to imitate you, as well as recording his correct and incorrect responses, should be continued until the 10-minute treatment time has ended.
5. After the session, add up the number of correct and incorrect responses. Then calculate and record the percent of correct imitative responses on the child's chart and compare his/her progress with the previous sessions.
6. The treatment phase should continue until the child reaches 90 percent or above correct imitations for three consecutive sessions.

If the child initially does not respond to your instructions to "Do this," you should use a *prompting procedure*. Prompting helps the child learn what the desirable target behavior is. First you should give your instruction, "[Name], do this," and show the response to be imitated. Then you should gently assist the child in performing the desired behavior. Upon completing the behavior, he should be rewarded and praised as if he had actually performed the behavior by himself. The next time, he should be allowed to try the response by himself. If he does not perform the behavior, prompting should again take place—though with a lessened grasp on the child. Reward should again follow this behavior. Prompting is continued until the child learns what has to be done in the situation. Most important, however, is to make sure that you lessen your assistance as the child progresses. He should have ample opportunity to perform the response by himself in the amount of time alloted. After awhile you will notice that the child will make the desired response exactly as you performed it—although it may take a number of sessions.

## ADDITIONAL COMMENTS

1. If possible, you should try to avoid presenting the imitative responses in the same order in each session.
2. A suggested tally sheet for imitation training appears in Table 9.
3. After the child has reached 90 percent or above correct imitations, you may want to begin teaching him more complex imitations. A few more complex imitations are listed here:

Stand up and sit down
Stand up and twirl around, sit down
Stand up, jump up and down, sit down
Stand up, walk to wall, tap wall with hand, sit back down in chair
Stand up and move chair back and forth, sit down
Stand up, go to door, touch door with one hand, go back to chair and sit down

## Table 9
### Tally Sheet For Imitation Training

+ = child imitated behavior and was reinforced
O = child did not imitate behavior
A = child attempted to imitate, but did not respond as accurately as in the past, therefore <u>no</u> reinforcement
S = (shaping) child attempted to imitate and was reinforced since response was more accurate than in the past

Child's name:_____
Date:_____
Session no.:_____

| | Trial 1 | Trial 2 | Trial 3 |
|---|---|---|---|
| 1. Raise both arms | | | |
| 2. Place hands on chest | | | |
| 3. Place hands on knees | | | |
| 4. Touch nose with one hand | | | |
| 5. Touch stomach with both hands | | | |
| 6. Touch ears with both hands | | | |
| 7. Place hands over eyes | | | |
| 8. Place both hands on top of head | | | |
| 9. Stretch both hands to the sides | | | |
| 10. Protrude tongue | | | |
| 11. Clap hands | | | |
| 12. Touch elbow with hand | | | |
| 13. Nod head | | | |
| 14. Tap chair | | | |
| 15. Stamp feet | | | |

## PROGRAM FOR INDEPENDENT EATING

Make sure that you use only foods that the child likes. If he/she is not used to receiving food from a spoon, spend a couple of days feeding him with a spoon. Throughout the program, praise the child for his progress. Make sure that you have made up a chart to graph the child's progress. The vertical line should state "Number of Steps" and the horizontal line, "Sessions."

1. Put the child's hand around the handle portion of the spoon and gently wrap your hand over his.
2. Assist the child in scooping the food and bringing the food to his mouth. Scoop food in a motion toward the child.
3. After the child receives the food, continue to hold his hand gently and direct his hand (and the spoon) back to the food.
4. Repeat steps 2 and 3.
5. While repeating steps 2 and 3, gradually begin to loosen your grip on the child's hand just before he puts the food in his mouth. Maintain this loose grip until after the child has received the food, then return his hand(spoon) to the food with the original amount of guidance.
6. Repeating steps 2 and 3, gradually loosen your grip on the child's hand just after he puts the food on his spoon. *Don't let go of his hand, just loosen your grip.* Maintain the loose grip until after the child has received the food, then redirect his hand and the spoon to the food with the original amount of guidance.
7. Repeat step 6, but in addition loosen your grip on his hand when you return his hand to the plate.
8. Repeat step 6, except loosen your grip even more when you return his hand to the plate. *Don't let go of his hand.*
9. Repeat step 8 except also loosen your grip even more just before he places the spoon in his mouth.
10. Repeat step 9, except this time let go of his hand completely just as the spoon enters his mouth. Retake his

hand with your loose grip *immediately after* he receives the food in his mouth.

11. Repeat step 10 except now place your hand just under his wrist *immediately before* he places the spoon in his mouth. Again, there should be no support while the spoon is in his mouth. Retake his hand with the loose grip and bring it back to the plate.

12. Repeat step 11, except move your hand under the child's wrist about three-quarters of the way up between the plate and his mouth.

13. Repeat step 12 except move your hand under the child's wrist about halfway between the "scoop" and his mouth.

14. Repeat step 13 except move your hand under the child's wrist about one-quarter of the way up between the plate and his mouth.

15. Repeat step 14 except move your hand under the child's forearm about three-quarters of the way between the plate and his mouth.

16. Repeat step 15 with your hand under his forearm about half of the way.

17. Repeat step 15 with your hand under his forearm about one quarter of the way.

18. Repeat step 17 except move your hand to the child's wrist after the food enters his mouth and then guide his hand back to the plate.

19. Repeat step 18 except place your hand under his forearm after the food enters the mouth. At this point, there should be firm pressure on the child's hand only when scooping the food. There should only be gentle forearm pressure for all other movements.

20. Repeat step 19 except move your hand to the child's wrist while he is scooping food. (You may have to gently guide him at first by grasping his hand.)

21. Repeat step 20 except move your hand to just under the child's elbow *immediately after* he scoops the food. After he receives the food, keep your hand under his elbow, guiding the spoon back to the plate.

22. Repeat step 21 except let go of the child's hand and arm completely about three-quarters of the way up from the scoop to his mouth. Continue guiding the return of the spoon to the food by placing your hand under his elbow.
23. Repeat step 22 except let go of the child's hand and arm half way between the scoop and his mouth.
24. Repeat step 23 except let go of the child's hand and arm one-quarter of the way between the scoop and his mouth.
25. Repeat step 24 but let go completely just after he makes the scoop. You may have to touch his hand gently to signal him to move the spoon to his mouth. His return to the plate should still be elbow guided.
26. Repeat step 25 except place your hand on the child's elbow while he's scooping.
27. Repeat step 26 except let go of the child's elbow on the return trip to the plate. (You may have to touch his hand gently to signal him to return spoon to food.)
28. Repeat step 27 except let go of the child's elbow completely. (You may have to guide child's hand at various points at first.) As the child continues to practice this step, gradually remove any prompting.

If the child drops the spoon at any point after he has held the spoon without assistance (step 11), the food and then the child should be immediately removed from the table. One hour later, the child should be given another opportunity to feed himself using this program.

Chart on your graph the last step that the child successfully completed at the end of each session.

ADDITIONAL COMMENTS

1. While using this program it is a good idea to use a bib which has a pouchlike lip at the bottom. This type of bib usually catches most of the food which spills out of the spoon.

2. If the child has repeated difficulty holding the spoon over a number of sessions, you may want to consider modifying the spoon's shape to further help him. For example, you can enlarge the handle of the spoon by wrapping adhesive tape around it. Then, as the child develops skill in holding the spoon, you can gradually remove some of the tape until he is again using a spoon with a "normal" handle. Other modified spoons are available commercially from medical supply stores that sell prosthetic devices. *If at all possible, you should only use a modified spoon on a temporary basis.* As the child develops expertise in using the modified spoon, you should gradually begin introducing him to the use of a normal spoon.

## PROGRAM FOR INDEPENDENT DRESSING: PANTS

Use loose fitting pants with an elasticized waist. Throughout the program, praise the child for any progress. Also, reward the child at each step with small amounts of his favorite food or drink. You will also need a chart to record the child's progress. The vertical line should state "Number of Steps" and the horizontal line, "Sessions."

1. Place pants completely on the child.
2. Pull pants up to *just below* the child's waist. Place your hands gently over the child's hands on either side of his pants and help him pull up his pants as you say, "[Name], pull up your pants." Praise the child for pulling up his pants.
3. Repeat step 2 except gently move your hands to his wrists.
4. Repeat step 2 except move your hands to his forearms to gently guide him.
5. Repeat step 2 except remove your hands from the child's forearms *(you may have to gently prompt him at first on this and later steps)*.
6. Pull pants up to the child's hips. Then have him pull the pants up the rest of the way. Remember to say to him, "Pull up your pants," and to praise him when he is successful.
7. Pull pants up to the child's knees. Then have him pull the pants up the rest of the way.
8. Have the child sit down with the pants up to his knees. Then have him stand up and pull his pants up the rest of the way. Remember to say, "Pull up your pants," and to praise him.
9. Have the child sit down. Place the pants *just over* his feet up to his ankles. Have him pull the pants up to his knees. Then have him stand up and pull the pants up the rest of the way.
10. Have the child sit down. Place the pants *just over* his toes. Have him pull the pants up to his knees. Then have him stand up and pull them up the rest of the way.

11. Have the child sit down. Place one of the child's feet into one of the pant legs until his toes show. Then have him place his other foot through the other pant leg and pull the pants up to his knees, then stand up and pull the pants up the rest of the way.

12. Have the child sit down. Place the pants in front of the child with the opening of one pant leg just touching the toes of one foot. Then have him first pull the pant leg up until his toes show, then place his second foot in the other pant leg, then pull them up to his knees, and stand up and pull them up the rest of the way.

13. Have the child sit down. Place the pants in front of the child. Have him grab the pants with his hands on both sides of the pants, place one foot through one pant leg, then the other foot through the other pant leg, pull them up to his knees, and stand up and pull them up the rest of the way.

14. Repeat step 13.

*Remember* to praise the child each time he successfully completes a step and to say to him, "[Name], pull up your pants" right before he begins to pull his pants up. You may have to prompt the child a few times at various points to help him completely learn a particular step. Chart on your graph the last step that the child successfully completed at the end of each session.

## PROGRAM FOR INDEPENDENT DRESSING: SHIRT

Use a loose fitting, short-sleeve T-shirt. (It is a good idea to use initially a shirt that is bigger than the child's normal size.) Throughout the program, praise the child for any progress. Also, reward the child at each step with small amounts of his favorite food or drink. You will also need a chart to record the child's progress. The vertical line should state "Number of Steps" and the horizontal line, "Sessions."

1. Place the shirt completely on the child.
2. Repeat step 1 except pull the shirt down to stomach level. Place your hands gently over the child's hands on either side of his shirt and help him pull his shirt down as you say, "[Name], put on your shirt." Praise the child for pulling down his shirt.
3. Repeat step 2 except gently move your hands to his wrist and guide him in pulling down his shirt.
4. Repeat step 2 except gently move your hands to his forearms and continue to gently guide him.
5. Repeat step 2 except remove your hands completely from the child's forearms (you may have to prompt him gently at first on this and later steps until he masters grasping and pulling down the shirt). Remember to say, "Put on your shirt."
6. Repeat step 5 except have the child pull down the shirt from midway between his stomach and chest.
7. Have the child pull down the shirt from chest level.
8. Have the child pull down the shirt from just below the armpits.
9. Have the child pull down the shirt from just over the back of the shoulders (the front of the shirt should be over his chest region).
10. Have the child pull down the shirt from just above the back of the neck. This can be accomplished by first having the child slowly swing his arms to his sides, then having him bring his arms back to the front of the shirt, and finally pulling it down.
11. Have the child pull down the shirt from the back of the

head. (This can be accomplished by having the child grab the neck region of the shirt and pull it down to his shoulders; then have him repeat step 10. The child should still have both arms through the sleeves of the shirt. *You may have to guide him gently through this and later steps.*)

12. Have the child pull down the shirt from the top of his head.

13. Have the child pull down the shirt from the front of his head (the child should now have both arms through the sleeves of the shirt, and the shirt should be across the child's upper arm region).

14. Have the child grab the waist opening of the T-shirt at the back and bring the T-shirt to the front of his head; then have him repeat step 13.

15. Have the child's arms placed three-quarters of the way through the sleeve. Have him push his arms through and then repeat step 14.

16. Have the child's arms placed half way through the sleeve. Have him push his arms through and then repeat step 14.

17. Have the child's arms placed one-quarter of the way through the sleeve. Have him push his arms through and then repeat step 14.

18. Place the shirt with the child's hands just at the arm opening. Have him push his arms all the way through and then repeat step 14.

19. Place the shirt with one of the child's arms just inside the shirt (shirt should be situated at child's chest region) and the other hand already through sleeve at forearm region. Have the child get one hand through the sleeve and then push both hands through and repeat step 14.

20. Place the shirt with one of the child's arms not inside the shirt (shirt should be at stomach region) and the other hand already through sleeve at forearm region. Have the child get one hand through the sleeve and push both hands through and then repeat step 14.

21. Hold the shirt out in front of the child and guide him in

placing one of his arms through a sleeve to the forearm; then encourage him to repeat step 20.

22. Have the child hold the shirt open at the waist so that he can insert one arm into the shirt and push it through the sleeve to his forearm; then have him repeat step 20.
23. Have the child lift up the back of the shirt at the waist to make an opening at the bottom of the T-shirt. Insert one arm and repeat step 22.
24. Have the child pick up the T-shirt from the table or chair and repeat step 23.

Remember to say, "[Name], put on your shirt," and to praise the child each time he successfully completes a step and puts on his shirt. You may have to prompt the child a few times at various points to help him develop expertise in putting on his shirt.

Chart on your graph the last step that the child successfully completed at the end of each session.

After he has mastered putting on a large T-shirt, introduce a slightly smaller T-shirt and encourage him to put this T-shirt on. Upon meeting with success, you should gradually proceed in having him put on T-shirts which are closer to (and then finally) his size.

## PROGRAM FOR INDEPENDENT DRESSING: SOCKS

Use loose-fitting socks. Throughout the program, praise the child for any progress. Also, reward the child at each step with small amounts of his favorite food or drink. You also need a chart to record the child's progress. The vertical line should state "Number of Steps" and the horizontal line, "Sessions."

1. While the child is sitting, place one sock completely on him.
2. Pull a sock up to just above his ankle. Place your hands gently over the child's hands on either side of the sock and help him pull up his sock as you say, "[Name], put on your socks." Praise the child for pulling up his sock.
3. Repeat step 2 except this time gently move your hand to his wrist and then help him pull up his sock.
4. Repeat step 2 except move your hands to his forearm and gently guide him.
5. Repeat step 2 except remove your hands completely from the child's forearm. (You may have to prompt him at first on this and later steps.)
6. Pull the sock up to the child's ankle region. Say to him, "Put on your socks." (You may have to prompt him and gently guide him in completing this activity.)
7. Repeat step 6 except have the child pull up the sock from just below his ankle.
8. Repeat step 6 except have the child pull up the sock from just above the heel.
9. Repeat step 6 except have the child pull up the sock from just below the heel.
10. Repeat step 6 except have the child pull up the sock from the middle of his foot.
11. Repeat step 6 except have the child pull up the sock from just above the toes.
12. Repeat step 6 except have the child pull up the sock from the toes.
13. While the child is holding the sock, have him place his toes in the sock opening; repeat step 12.

14. Have the child pick up the sock with both hands and bring the sock to his toes; repeat step 13.
15. With the sock in front of the child, instruct him to put on his sock; repeat step 15. (You may have to prompt the child a few times at various points to help him complete the activity.)

Remember to say "[Name], put on your socks," and to praise the child each time he successfully completes a step. Chart on your graph the last step that the child successfully completes at the end of each session.

## PROGRAM FOR INDEPENDENT DRESSING: TYING SHOES[7]

Use a shoe with a shoestring which is *longer than average* for the child's shoes. Each half of the shoestring should be a different color (e.g., red and white). Throughout the program, praise the child for any progress. Also reward the child at each step with small amounts of his/her favorite food or drink. Make sure that you chart the child's progress; the vertical line should state "Number of Steps" and the horizontal line, "Sessions."

1. Place the shoe on a table in front of the child. The heel of the shoe should be directly in front of the child and the toe of the shoe away from the child. (The child should be seated.)
2. Help the child take the left (red) shoestring and place it to the left of the front of the toe of the shoe. (You may have to prompt him at first on this and later steps. If the child prefers handling the right shoestring first, adjust the program to his preference.)
3. Next, help the child take the right (white) shoestring and place it to the right of the front of the toe of the shoe.
4. Repeat steps 2 and 3. Next, have the child pick up the red shoestring, cross it over the white string, and place it down to the right of the white string.
5. Repeat step 4. Then have the child pick up the white string and bring it down toward the center of the shoe so that the tip of the string is touching the tongue of the shoe. (Make sure the strings are still crossed.)
6. Repeat step 5. Then have the child place the white string under the red string (beneath the crossed strings) and pull it toward the toe of the shoe.
7. Repeat step 6. Next, have the child pick up the red and white strings and pull them out towards the sides away from each other (red to right, white to left), and then have him place them down.

---

[7]This program is based in part on a film by Meyerson, L. (Producer). *Rewards and reinforcements in learning*. Scottsdale, Ariz.: Behavior Modification Productions, 1969.

8. Repeat step 7. Have the child pick up the middle of the red string and bring it to the tongue of the shoe (a large loop should result from this action).
9. Repeat step 8. Then have the child pick up the middle of this white string and bring it to the tongue of the shoe (a second large loop should result from this action).
10. Repeat step 9. Next, have the child pick up the tip of the white loop with his right hand and place it across the red loop. Then have the child continue holding the white loop with his right hand.
11. Repeat step 10. Have the child pick up the tip of the red loop with his left hand and place it across the white loop. (Make sure the loops are still crossed.) The child should continue holding both loops.
12. Repeat step 11. Have the child place the red loop under the white loop and pull it away from the center of the shoe, and then put both loops down.
13. Repeat step 12. Then have the child pick up the red and white loops and pull them slowly out toward the sides away from each other. He should then put them down.

Remember to praise the child each time he successfully completes a step. You may have to prompt the child a few times at various points to help him complete each step. You may also have to help him practice these steps *many times* before he develops expertise in tying his shoes. Next, have him practice on shoes which have almost normal length shoestrings. Make sure you offer guidance when it seems necessary and that you reward him for being successful. Gradually withdraw your help. Next, have him practice on shoes with normal length shoestrings, assisting him when necessary, until he develops complete expertise. Finally, have him practice on shoes that are on his feet, assisting him when necessary, until he has mastered tying his own shoes.

Chart on your graph the last step that the child successfully completes at the end of each session.

An alternative way of teaching the child to tie shoes is to reverse the above program and first teach him to tie a bow. Using this reversal procedure, you would guide the child through steps

1–12 of the program. Then you would help him do part of step 13 and encourage him to do the rest on his own. You would then reward him when he is finished. Next, you would guide him through the first 12 steps again, and when you reached the last step he would be encouraged to do more of this step on his own. Again, you would reward him when he was finished. This procedure of backward chaining would be continued throughout all the remaining steps until the child can begin step 1 on his own and perform all of the succeeding steps on his own. In every instance, you would only reward the child when he finished step 13.

## PROGRAM FOR INDEPENDENT DRESSING: PUTTING ON A ZIPPERED COAT

Use a loose-fitting jacket which has an easily workable zipper. Throughout the program, praise the child for any progress. Also reward the child at each step with small amounts of his favorite food or drink. Make sure that you chart the child's progress. The vertical line should state "Number of Steps" and the horizontal line, "Sessions."

1. Place the jacket completely on the child. Do not zipper the jacket.
2. Place the jacket on the child, except have the child's right arm placed only three-quarters of the way through the sleeve. Say to the child, "[Name], put on your coat," and gently guide him in pushing his hand through the sleeve opening and placing the coat completely on his shoulders.
3. Place the jacket on the child, except have the child's right arm placed only halfway through the sleeve. Say to him, "[Name], put on your coat," and gently guide him in pushing his hand through the sleeve opening and placing the coat on his shoulders. (Begin gradually to reduce your guidance.)
4. Place the jacket on the child, except have child's right arm placed only one-quarter of the way through the sleeve. Then have him push his arm through the rest of the way, placing the coat on his shoulders. (Again, gradually withdraw your assistance.)
5. Place the child's right hand just at the arm opening of the jacket. Have him push his arm all the way through. (Again, you may have to guide him at certain points.)
6. Repeat step 5, except this time have the child's left arm placed three-quarters of the way through the sleeve. Say to him "[Name], put on your coat," and guide him, if necessary, in putting his coat on.
7. Repeat step 5, except this time have the child's left arm placed halfway through the sleeve. Then encourage him to put on his coat. (Again, you may have to guide him at certain points.)

8. Repeat step 5, except this time place the child's left arm one-quarter of the way through the sleeve. Then encourage him to put on his coat.

9. Repeat step 5, except this time have the child's left hand just at the arm opening of the jacket. Then have him push all the way through until the coat is on both shoulders.

10. Place the jacket front side up (unzipped) on top of a table (or on a chair) and say to the child, "[Name], put on your coat." Then gently guide the child through steps 1 through 9. Practice this five consecutive times, gradually withdrawing your assistance. If the child has any difficulty with a particular step, review the step with him until he can successfully put on his coat.

Once the child has learned to put his coat on without continued assistance, you should begin to teach him how to zipper his coat. Again, praise the child for any progress. Also reward the child at each step with small amounts of his favorite food or drink. Make sure you use a coat that has a zipper that moves easily.

11. Let the child put on his coat to your statement "[Name], put on your coat." Then you should pull the zipper all the way up.

12. Let the child put on his coat. Then pull the zipper up to just above his chest level. Place your hand gently over the child's hand and help him pull up the zipper as you say, "[Name], pull up your zipper."

13. Let the child put on his coat. Then pull the zipper up to just above his chest level. Gently place your hand over the child's hand until he grasps the zipper. Then move your hand to his wrist and guide him in pulling up the zipper as you say, "[Name], pull up your zipper."

14. Repeat step 13 except move your hand to his forearm to guide him.

15. Repeat step 13 except this time remove your hand from the child's forearm (you may have to prompt him at first on this and later steps). Make sure you say, "[Name], pull up your zipper."

16. Let the child put on his coat. Then pull the zipper to his chest level and encourage him to pull the zipper up the rest of the way. (Again, you may have to prompt him a few times.)
17. Repeat step 16 except this time have the child pull up the zipper from midway between his waist and his chest.
18. Repeat step 16 except this time have him pull up his zipper from just above his waist level.
19. Repeat step 16 except have the child pull up his zipper from waist level. (If the child's coat goes beyond his waist level, he should next be encouraged to pull up the zipper from his hip region.)
20. Repeat step 16 except have the child pull the zipper all the way up from the bottom of the zipper.
21. Let the child put on his coat. Then help him grasp the two parts of the unhooked zipper, one part in each hand, and then help him connect them. Then have him zip the coat up all the way, to your statement "Pull up your zipper."
22. Repeat Step 21, except this time gradually withdraw your assistance in helping him connect the two parts of the zipper. Do not hold his hands too firmly in guiding him. Make sure you praise him when he is successful.
23. Repeat step 21, except this time place your hands over his wrists and assist him in connecting the two parts of the zipper. As soon as the zipper is connected, withdraw your help and tell him to "Pull up your zipper." Make sure you praise him for being successful.
24. Repeat step 21, except this time place your hands on his forearms and gently guide him in connecting the two parts of the zipper.
25. Repeat step 21, except this time encourage him to connect the two parts of the zipper with little if any assistance from you. (You may in the beginning have to guide him. Then gradually withdraw all your assistance until he is completely successful by himself.) You may have to practice this step a number of times before the child develops expertise in zipping up the zipper.

Remember to say, "[Name], put on your coat [pull up your zipper]" and to praise the child each time he successfully completes a step. You may have to prompt the child a few times at various points to help him complete the activity.

Chart on your graph the last step that the child successfully completes at the end of each session.

## PROGRAM FOR INDEPENDENT WALKING[8]

Before initiating this program, the child should be seen by a physician for a thorough examination to determine if there is any physical reason why he cannot (or should not) learn to walk. Throughout the program, praise the child for any progress. Also reward the child at each step with small amounts of his favorite food or drink, as well as social praise. The food and drink should be placed directly in the child's mouth. You will need a graph to chart the child's progress. The vertical line should state "Number of Steps" and the horizontal line, "Sessions."

MATERIALS NEEDED

Two sturdy wooden chairs with spaced slot backs and weights (e.g., a 50-pound bag of sand) anchored to each chair. The chairs should be back to back in the middle of a room. The room should be well lighted and devoid of any distractions for the child. Two therapists are needed for this program, and they should sit on the chairs so that they are facing one another.

1. Place the child between the two chairs on the floor in a sitting position. (There should be a distance of about two feet between the two chair backs.) Say to the child, "[Name], stand up," and gently guide his hands to the first rung of one of the chairs. Then, while he is holding onto the rung, gently help him pull himself up by lifting him under each arm. (Both therapists should participate in helping the child stand up—each therapist holding one side of the child.)
2. Repeat step 1 except this time guide the child's hands to the next rung on the same chair while saying to the child, "[Name], stand up." Then help him stand up

---

[8]This program is based on an article by Meyerson, L., Kerr, N., & Michael, J. L. Behavior modification in rehabilitation. In S. W. Bijou &D. M. Baer eds., *Child development: Readings in experimental analysis.* New York: Appleton-Century-Crofts, 1967; and a study by Morris, R. J., & O'Neill, J. H. Establishing independent walking in retarded children. Unpublished study. Syracuse University, 1974.

(make sure he is still holding on to the rung). The therapists may have to hold the child's hands in order to help him maintain his balance.

3. Repeat step 1 except guide the child's hands to the top rung and gently help him pull himself up. Make sure he is holding on to the rung. If necessary, the therapists should hold the child's hands on the rung to help him maintain his balance.

4. Repeat step 3. Make sure that he is holding on to the chair with both hands. (The therapists may have to hold their hands over the child's hands to help him maintain his balance.)

5. While the child is standing between the two therapists and holding on to the top rung of the first therapist's chair, the second therapist should then say, "[Name], come to me," and gently guide the child's hand across to the top rung on the opposite chair. After the child places his hand on the second chair, the second therapist should reward him with his favorite food. (If the child drops down to the floor, repeat step 3, rewarding the child only after he successfully completes step 3.)

6. Repeat step 5 for the child's other hand (the child's upper body should now be facing the second therapist. The second therapist should also gently guide the child's feet and torso so that they are facing his/her chair.

7. Repeat steps 5 and 6 using the first therapist so that the child can transfer back to that chair.

8. Repeat steps 5 through 7, gradually withdrawing the physical guidance by the therapists. (Both therapists should continue to say, "[Name], come to me," before each transfer from one chair to the other, and continue to reward the child with verbal praise and food and drink for successful transfers). You may have to prompt the child at various points to help him learn how to transfer. Make sure that each therapist says, "[Name], come to me," only when he/she wants the child to transfer in his/her direction.

9. Repeat steps 5 through 7 until the child completes 10 consecutive successful unassisted transfers.

10. Increase the distance between the chairs to 30 inches. Then repeat steps 5 through 7 until the child has made 10 consecutive successful unassisted transfers.

11. Increase the distance between the chairs to 36 inches. Then repeat steps 5 through 7 until the child has made 10 consecutive successful unassisted transfers. (If the child can no longer reach the other side by just stretching out his arms you may have to provide some support for him until he learns to move his feet to aid him in reaching the other chair.)

12. Increase the distance between the chairs to 42 inches. Then repeat steps 5 through 7 until the child has made 10 consecutive successful unassisted transfers. (Once again, you may have to guide the child at first to help him learn to move his feet.)

13. Increase the distance between the chairs to 48 inches. Then repeat steps 5 through 7 until the child has made 10 consecutive successful unassisted transfers.

14. Increase the distance between the chairs to 54 inches. Then repeat steps 5 through 7 until the child has made 10 consecutive successful unassisted transfers.

15. Increase the distance between the chairs to 60 inches. Then repeat steps 5 through 7 until the child has made 10 consecutive successful unassisted transfers.

16. Turn the chairs around so that they are facing each other. The chairs should be about 60 inches apart. The therapists should sit in a normal way on the chairs. The child should be placed next to one therapist. The other therapist should then say, "[Name], come to me." When the child walks to the therapist, he should be rewarded and praised. The second therapist should then say, "[Name], come to me," and also reward the child for walking to the therapist. (You may have to prompt the child at various points to help him walk from one therapist to the other.) Repeat this step until the child has made 10 consecutive successful unassisted transfers.

17. Increase the distance between the chairs to 72 inches, and repeat step 16 until the child has made 10 consecutive successful unassisted transfers.

18. Increase the distance between the chairs to 84 inches, and repeat step 16 until the child has made 10 consecutive successful unassisted transfers.
19. Increase the distance between the chairs to 96 inches, and repeat step 16 until the child has made 10 consecutive successful unassisted transfers. (By this time the child should be walking independently and freely rewarded for walking around.)

Remember to praise and reward the child each time he successfully transfers from one chair to the other. Gentle guidance is often helpful in aiding the child in the initial learning of a particular step.

Chart on your graph the last step that the child successfully completes at the end of each session.

## PROGRAM FOR INDEPENDENT TOOTHBRUSHING

Use a toothbrush which is appropriate for the child's size (you should check with a dentist to determine whether the child should use a soft, medium, or hard toothbrush, as well as what the configuration of the toothbrush should be). Throughout the program, praise the child for any progress. Also, reward the child at the end of the session with an appropriate amount of his favorite food or drink. You should also chart the child's progress. The vertical line should state "Number of Steps" and the horizontal line, "Sessions." (*Note:* This program assumes that the child can grasp and hold a toothbrush and toothpaste by himself.)

1. Bring the child to the washroom and place his toothbrush and a tube of open toothpaste directly in front of him. Tell the child, "Pick up the tube of toothpaste and place some toothpaste on the toothbrush. Then, place the toothpaste back down." If the child follows this instruction, go to step 10. If he *does not* follow this instruction, gently cover his hands with yours and guide him in spreading the toothpaste on the toothbrush and then place the toothpaste down (the toothbrush should be placed in his preferred hand).
2. Repeat step 1, except loosen your grip on the child's hands.
3. Repeat step 1, except loosen your grip even more, but *do not let go of his hand.*
4. Repeat step 1, except place your hand just under the child's wrist *immediately* before he places the toothpaste on the toothbrush. Continue guiding him from this position and praising him (you may have to grasp one of his hands initially to help him spread the toothpaste).
5. Repeat step 1, except move your hand down toward the middle of the child's arm. Continue guiding him and praising him for making progress.
6. Repeat step 5, except remove your hands from his arms immediately before he places the toothpaste down (you may have to guide him occasionally on this and later steps).

7. Repeat step 5, except remove your hands from his arms immediately before he finishes putting the toothpaste on the toothbrush.

8. Repeat step 5, except remove your hands just as he begins placing the toothpaste on the toothbrush.

9. Repeat step 1 (you may have to gently guide him at times until he develops mastery of this skill).

10. After the child successfully completes step 1 or step 9, he should be told, "Now I want you to brush your teeth." If the child does not follow this instruction, then you should gently cover his hand with yours and guide his hand through the following sequence:

    a. turn the water on in the wash basin to a moderate degree and then bring his hand slowly toward his mouth,

    b. touch the toothbrush bristles to his teeth and move the toothbrush up and down on the outer surface of his front teeth for 5 to 10 seconds (avoid placing undue pressure on the child's gums),

    c. then gently move the toothbrush to one side of the child's mouth (the child's preferred side) and brush this side for 5 to 10 seconds in an up-and-down motion,

    d. then gently move the toothbrush to the other side of his mouth and brush this side for 5 to 10 seconds in an up-and-down motion,

    e. then gently move the toothbrush to the bottom surfaces of his top teeth on his preferred side and brush them for 5 to 10 seconds,

    f. then gently move the toothbrush to the bottom surfaces of his top teeth on the other side and brush them for 5 to 10 seconds,

    g. then guide his hand and toothbrush to the upper surfaces of his bottom teeth on his preferred side and brush them for 5 to 10 seconds,

    h. then guide his hand and toothbrush to the upper surfaces of his bottom teeth on the other side and brush them for 5 to 10 seconds,

    i. then guide the child in brushing the inside surfaces of his bottom teeth,

    j. then guide him in brushing the inside surfaces of his top teeth,

    k. then guide the toothbrush out of his mouth and back toward the wash basin,

    l. place the toothbrush under the water, rinse it off, and put it down,

    m. then encourage the child to spit out the toothpaste which has remained in his mouth,

    n. then guide him in picking up a cup, filling it with water, rinsing out his mouth, and placing the cup back down,

    o. and, finally, guide him in turning off the water and wiping his face and hands with a towel.

11. Repeat the sequence presented in step 10, except loosen your grip on the child's hands.

12. Repeat the sequence in step 10, except loosen your grip even more. *Do not let go of his hand.*

13. Repeat the sequence in step 10, except place your hand just under the child's wrist *immediately* before he places the toothbrush in his mouth. Continue guiding him from this position and praising him for doing well. Retake his hand after he is finished using the toothbrush in his mouth.

14. Repeat the sequence in step 10, except move your hand just under his wrist about three-quarters of the way up between the wash basin and his mouth. Retake his hand after he is finished using the toothbrush in his mouth.

15. Repeat the sequence in step 10, except move your hand under his wrist about half way up between the wash basin and his mouth. Retake his hand after he is finished using the toothbrush in his mouth.

16. Repeat the sequence in step 10, except move your hand under his wrist about one-quarter of the way up between the wash basin and his mouth. Leave your hand in this position after he is finished with the toothbrush in his mouth (you may have to regrasp his hand occasion-

ally to aid him in rinsing the toothbrush).

17. Repeat the sequence in step 10, except move your hand under the child's forearm about three-quarters of the way up between the wash basin and his mouth. Leave your hand in this position after he is finished with the toothbrush in his mouth (again, you may have to guide him gently through the remainder of the sequence).

18. Repeat the sequence in step 10, except move your hand under the child's forearm about half way up between the wash basin and his mouth. (Again, leave your hand in this position throughout the remainder of the sequence, although you may have to retake his hand at certain times to further guide him).

19. Repeat the sequence in step 10, except move your hand under the child's forearm about one-quarter of the way between the wash basin and his mouth. Leave your hand in this position throughout the remainder of the program.

20. Repeat step 10 (you may have to gently guide the child through various parts of the sequence until he develops expertise in brushing his teeth).

21. Repeat steps 1 and 10 (again, you may have to guide the child occasionally until he develops complete mastery of these skills).

Remember to praise the child each time he completes a step and successfully brushes his teeth. Chart on your graph the last step that the child successfully completes at the end of each session. After the child has mastered brushing his teeth, you may want to begin teaching him how to take off and replace the cap to the toothpaste, as well as how to use dental floss. Also, be sure to bring the child to the dentist for regular check-ups.

## PROGRAM FOR INDEPENDENT FACE WASHING

Throughout the program, praise the child for any progress. Also, reward him at the end of each session with an appropriate amount of his favorite food or drink. You should also chart the child's progress. The vertical line should state "Number of Steps" and the horizontal line, "Sessions."

1. Bring the child to the bathroom and stand him in front of the sink. Say to him, "[Name], wash your face." Then turn the water on. (This program assumes that the child is familiar with having water on his face. If he is not familiar with this, the therapist should take the time to place small amounts of water gently over his face until he feels comfortable with having the water on his face.)

2. Bring the child to the bathroom and have him stand in front of the sink. Say to him, "[Name], wash your face." Then guide him in turning on the appropriate amount of hot and cold water to achieve a warm water temperature. Assist him in cupping his hands, in bringing his cupped hands under the water, and then in patting his face with the water (this process should be performed in one continuous motion).

3. Repeat step 2. After the child pats his face with the water, continue to hold his cupped hands and gently direct them back to the water.

4. Repeat step 3.

5. While repeating step 3, gradually begin to loosen your grip on the child's cupped hands just before he places the water on his face. Maintain the loose grip until after he has placed the water on his face; then return his hands to the water with the original amount of guidance.

6. Repeat step 3, but this time gradually loosen your grip on the child's hand just after he gets water in his hands. Don't let go of his hands, merely loosen your grip. Maintain this loose grip until after he has patted his face with the water, then redirect his hands to the water with the original amount of guidance.

7. Repeat step 6, except also loosen your grip on his hands as you return his hands to the water.
8. Repeat step 7, except this time loosen your grip on his hands even more, without letting go of his hands entirely.
9. Repeat step 8, except let go of his hands *just as* he splashes the water on his face, retaking his hands with your loose grip *immediately after* he finishes splashing his face.
10. Repeat step 9, except place your hand just under his wrist *immediately before* he pats water on his face. There should be no support of his hands while he is splashing his face but you should retake his hands with the loose grip and bring them back to the water.
11. Repeat step 10, except move your hand under the child's wrist about three-quarters of the way between the water and his face.
12. Repeat step 10, except move your hand under the child's wrist about half way between the water and his face.
13. Repeat step 10, except move your hand under the child's wrist about one-quarter of the way between the water and his face.
14. Assist the child in cupping his hands and bringing his cupped hands under the water. Then, as you guide the child's hands (at the wrist) to his face, move your hand to his forearm about three-quarters of the way between the water and his face.
15. Repeat step 14, except move your hand under the child's forearm about half way between the water and his face.
16. Repeat step 14, except move your hand under the child's forearm about one-quarter of the way between the water and his face.
17. Repeat step 14, except this time move your hand to the child's wrist *right after* he splashes his face.
18. Repeat step 14, except place your hand under the child's forearm right after he splashes his face. (At this point there should be firm pressure on the child's hands

only as he begins to cup the water. Gentle forearm pressure should be present for all other movements.)

19. Repeat step 14, except move your hand to the child's wrist just as he is cupping his hands. (You may have to guide him gently at first by gripping his hands.)

20. Repeat step 14, except move your hand to just under the child's elbow just as he cups his hands. After this, continue to have your hand under his forearm and gently guide him through the other motions.

21. Repeat step 20, except let go of the child's forearm completely about three-quarters of the way from placing water in his hands. Continue guiding the return of his hands to the water by placing your hand under his elbow.

22. Repeat step 20, except let go of the child's hand and arm half way between the water and his face.

23. Repeat step 20, but let go of the child's hand and arm one-quarter of the way between the water and his face.

24. Repeat step 20, but let go completely just after the child places water in his hands. You may have to touch his hand gently to signal him to move his hands to his face. His return to the water should still be elbow guided.

25. Repeat step 20, except do not guide the child's arm back to the water. (You may have to prompt the child occasionally.)

Remember to say, "[Name], wash your face," and to praise the child for the successful completion of each step. Chart on your graph the last step that the child successfully completes at the end of each session.

If you wish to teach the child to wash his face with soap and/or a wash cloth, you can extend this program using the same graduated format. You can also apply this program (after minor modification) to teaching the child to wash other parts of his body (e.g., neck, underarms).

At the end of each session assist the child in turning off the water and in using a towel to dry his face and hands. As the child progresses, gradually withdraw your guidance in these activities — until he can perform them by himself.

## PROGRAM FOR INDEPENDENT HAIR COMBING

Make sure that you use a comb which can be easily handled by the child. Throughout the program praise the child for any progress. Also reward the child at each step with small amounts of his favorite food or drink. You will also need a chart to record the child's progress. The vertical line should state "Number of Steps" and the horizontal line, "Sessions." (*Note:* This program assumes that the child can grasp a comb.)

1. Pick up the comb and place it in the child's hand, cupping your hand over his. Say to the child, "[Name], comb your hair."
2. Repeat step 1 and guide the child's hand and comb to the child's hair.
3. Repeat step 2 (again saying, "[Name], comb your hair"); then, while holding his hand over the comb, comb the child's hair in accordance with your preference.
4. Repeat step 3 except slightly loosen your grip on the child's hand.
5. Repeat step 3 except loosen your grip even more.
6. Repeat step 3 except gradually move your hand to the child's wrist and continue guiding his hair combing.
7. Repeat step 6 except move your hand to the child's wrist. Loosen your grip slightly so that he can have the opportunity to move the comb.
8. Repeat step 6 except move your hand just under the child's elbow. Continue guiding him whenever it seems necessary.
9. Repeat step 8 except remove your guidance completely. (You may have to guide the child occasionally.)

Remember to say "[Name], comb your hair," and to praise the child each time he successfully completes a step. You may have to prompt the child a few times at various points to help him reach complete mastery.

Chart on your graph the last step that the child successfully completes at the end of each session.

## PROGRAM FOR COMMAND FOLLOWING: "COME TO ME"

Throughout the program, praise the child for any progress. Also, reward him at each step with small amounts of his favorite food or drink. Chart the child's progress. The vertical line should state "Number of Steps" and the horizontal line, "Sessions."

1. Stand face to face with the child at a distance of two feet. Say, "[Name], come to me!" At the same time, gesture to him that you want him to come to you by stretching out your arms in front of you and slowly bringing them back toward your chest. If the child does not come to you, repeat the command and reach for his forearms and slowly pull him toward you. Repeat this prompting procedure until he comes to you without assistance. (Although you should continue using gestures, you should gradually withdraw your assistance as the child progresses in coming to you on command. In this way, the child will learn to perform the behavior by himself.)

2. Repeat step 1, except stand three feet from the child. If he does not come to you, repeat the command and reach for his forearms and slowly pull him toward you. (Repeat this prompting procedure until the child comes to you without your assistance. Continue using gestures but gradually withdraw your prompting until he comes to you without any assistance.)

3. Repeat step 1, except stand four feet from the child. (If he does not come to you in response to your command, repeat the prompting procedure and then gradually withdraw your prompts until he comes to you without any assistance.)

4. Repeat step 1, except stand five feet away from the child. (If necessary, use the prompting procedure to assist the child in following your command. Be sure to withdraw your prompts gradually as the child learns to come to you.)

5. Repeat step 1, except stand six feet from the child. (If necessary, move toward the child and use the prompting procedure to bring him to you.)

6. Repeat step 1, except stand nine feet from the child. (You may have to use prompts at first in this and the remaining steps.)
7. Repeat step 1, except stand 12 feet from the child.
8. Repeat step 1, except stand 20 feet from the child (or at the opposite side of the room).

Remember to praise the child each time he shows even the slightest amount of progress. Chart on your graph the last step that the child successfully completes at the end of each session.

## PROGRAM FOR COMMAND FOLLOWING: "SIT DOWN"

For this program you will need a chair which is appropriate for the child's size. (The child should be able to sit comfortably in the chair with his feet touching the floor.) Throughout the program, praise the child for any progress. Also, reward him with small amounts of his favorite food or drink. You will also need a chart to record the child's progress. The vertical line should state "Number of Steps" and the horizontal line should state "Sessions."

1. Stand face to face with the child at a distance of two feet. Say, "[Name], sit down!" While you are saying the command, gesture to him to sit down — that is, outstretch your hands in front of you and move them downward toward the floor. If the child does not follow your command, say the command again and gently place your hands on his shoulders and assist him in sitting down. Repeat this prompting procedure (gradually withdrawing your assistance) until the child responds to your command without any prompting. (For some children you may have to help them learn to bend their knees before they can learn to sit down.)

2. Repeat step 1 except stand three feet away from the child. If he does not follow your command and gesture, place your hands on his shoulders and gently sit him down. Repeat the prompting procedure until he performs the behavior without any assistance.

3. Repeat step 1 except stand four feet from the child. If he does not respond to your command and gesture, repeat the command and the prompting procedure and then gradually withdraw your prompts until he follows your command without any help.

4. Repeat step 1 except stand six feet from the child. If he does not respond to your command and gesture, repeat the command and the prompting procedure by reaching over to him and gently sitting him down. Be sure to withdraw your assistance gradually as he learns to follow the command.

5. Repeat step 1 except stand twelve feet away. (If necessary, move toward the child and use the prompting procedure until he can follow the command without any prompting.)
6. Repeat step 1 except stand sixteen feet away (or at the opposite side of the room). You may have to use prompting until he performs the behavior without any assistance.

Remember to praise the child each time he successfully shows even the slightest amount of progress. Chart on your graph the last step that he successfully completes at the end of each session.

## PROGRAM FOR COMMAND FOLLOWING: "PUT THAT DOWN"

Stand the child next to a table (the table should be on his dominant side) and place a small box or object on the table. Throughout the program, praise the child for any progress. Also reward the child at each step with small amounts of his favorite food or drink. You will also need a chart to record the child's progress. The vertical line should state "Number of Steps" and the horizontal line, "Sessions."

1. Stand face to face with the child at a distance of two feet. Place the small box or object in the child's dominant hand. Say to him, "[Name], put that down!" While you are saying the command, gesture to him to put the box down—that is, point to the box in his hand and then point to the place where you want him to place it. If the child does not follow your command, repeat the command and then gently reach for his dominant hand and lead it down toward the table. Then slowly help him open his hand and assist him in placing the box on the table. Finally, gently guide his hand away from the table. Repeat this prompting procedure (gradually withdrawing your assistance) until the child responds to your command without any prompting.

2. Repeat step 1 except stand three feet away from the child. If he does not follow your command, reach for his dominant hand and gradually bring it down toward the table and help him place the box on the table. (Make sure you use the gesture when you give the command.) Repeat the prompting procedure until he performs the behavior without any assistance.

3. Repeat step 1, except stand five feet away. If he does not respond to your command and gesture, repeat the prompting procedure and then gradually withdraw your prompts until he follows your command without any help.

4. Repeat step 1, except stand eight feet away. (If necessary, move toward the child and use the prompting proce-

dure. Be sure to withdraw your assistance gradually as the child learns to place the box down.)

5. Repeat step 1, except stand 12 feet away. (If necessary, move toward the child and use the prompting procedure until he can follow the command without any prompting.)

6. Repeat step 1, except stand 16 feet away (or at the opposite side of the room). You may have to move toward the child and use prompting until he performs the behavior without any assistance.

Remember to praise the child each time he successfully shows even the slightest amount of progress. Chart on your graph the last step that the child successfully completes at the end of each session.

To help the child learn to follow this command when he is holding various types of objects, place different items in his hand and repeat step 6 of the program. Praise the child and reward him for successfully following your command.

## PROGRAM FOR REDUCING A CHILD'S FEAR[9]

This program assumes that the child is afraid of *something which can be seen* by the therapist (e.g., animals, elevators, darkness, strangers, going into the water in a swimming pool, high places). Throughout the program praise the child for any progress. You should also chart the child's progress. The vertical line of the chart should state "Number of Steps" and the horizontal line, "Sessions."

1. If you are uncertain what the child is afraid of, talk with him and help him describe exactly what he is afraid of. Then, identify the target behavior as clearly as possible. In order to use this program, you should be able to see the feared object.
2. In order to help the child overcome his fear, you should develop a graduated series of steps (hierarchy) toward the feared object — *starting with the least fearful step,* which the child is willing to make (and has no trouble making), and gradually moving down to the most fearful step that the child prefers not to make. *The development of the hierarchy is one of the most important steps in this program.* Make certain that it represents a very gradual gradation toward the feared object.
3. Write out the hierarchy steps on a sheet of paper and show them to a friend or colleague. This person should agree that the hierarchy represents a gradation toward the feared object. If there is some disagreement with a few of the steps in the hierarchy, modify those steps.
4. Number the vertical line of your chart to correspond to the number of steps in your hierarchy. The horizontal line should state "Sessions." Each session should last not

---

[9]This prescription is based on a study by Morris, R. J., & Morisano, E. The treatment of aquaphobia in retarded persons via contact desensitization. Unpublished study. Syracuse University, 1974; and a study by Morisano, E. R. A comparison of the effects of contact desensitization and symbolic modeling in the treatment of phobic retardates. Unpublished doctoral dissertation. Syracuse University, 1975.

more than 20 minutes, with two to five sessions per week (one session per day).

5. Expose the child to the first, least fearful step on the hierarchy. Tell the child that you are now going to perform the first step on the hierarchy (instead of using these words, you would just say what the first step is), and after you are finished the two of you will do the same activity again. Thus, after you *model* each step, you should *gradually ease* the child into performing that same step (with you participating, too). You should also *encourage* the child throughout his performance of the step, *praise* him for even the slightest progress, and *physically help* him to practice that step. After performing a particular step, the child should feel fairly confident that he can perform it again.

6. If the child successfully completes this first step, you should then proceed to the next step. Do not rush the child through any steps. Always model the step first, then encourage his participation, praise him, and physically help him perform the step. If the child does not successfully complete the first step, this indicates that the hierarchy is not graduated enough and/or you have not successfully identified the least fearful step which the child is willing to perform (and has no trouble performing).

7. At the end of a session, record the last step that the child has successfully completed. Chart his progress and praise him for his progress and show your happiness for the success he has made.

8. At the next session, start the child at the beginning of the hierarchy and proceed through the steps that he has already successfully completed. As the child repeatedly practices these earlier steps, gradually withdraw your modeling and physical help, although you should continue encouraging and praising him. When you reach the last step that the child successfully completed in the previous session, model that step again and then proceed with the rest of the procedure. *Before beginning a new session always review the earlier steps which have been successfully completed. Start the new session with the*

*last step that the child successfully completed in the previous session.*

9. If the child is hesitant to perform a particular step, or just refuses to perform a step, do not force the child. Go back a step and model it and then have the child perform the step. Then go to the next step and have the child imitate what you did (again, encouraging, praising, and assisting him). If the child still fails that step, go back to the last step that he successfully completed and have him repeat that step. Then, stop the session. *It is important to always end each session with the successful completion of a step.* If a child repeatedly fails a step, break it down into smaller graduated components and have the child perform each step as he would any other step on the hierarchy. To help you modify a step, you should also ask the child what about the failed step is difficult for him to perform. Then, adjust the particular step accordingly. At the next session, have the child go through those steps that he has already mastered, and then start the contact desensitization procedure on the last step that he successfully completed, followed by his exposure to the revised steps. Further modification of the steps and added therapist contact and reassurrance may be necessary.

Remember, always praise the child for any progress, and use modeling, encouragement, and physical help to assist him in mastering a particular step. *Never* require the child to do anything that he truly does not want to do. If the child is having difficulty progressing from one step to another, develop in-between steps to help him gradually progress to the next step.

## PROGRAM FOR TOILET TRAINING

This program assumes that the child can obey simple commands (e.g., "Sit down!"). It is advisable for the child to know how to pull down/up his pants and wash his hands. Throughout the program praise the child for any progress, and reward him with small amounts of his favorite food or drink. You should also keep a daily tally sheet of the child's progress and transfer this information to the child's chart at the end of each day. Circle "Number of Times" (wet/BM) on the vertical line and "Days" on the horizontal line. You will also need a potty chair appropriate for the child's size (for larger children you can use an insert for a normal commode or even the regular commode). When necessary, use a urine deflector for boys.

The daily tally sheet should resemble the observation sheet presented in Table 4 (Chapter 2) with the following modification: record a "+" when the child is dry, a "++" when the child has not had a bowel movement(BM), a "−" when the child is wet, a "−−" when the child has had a BM. Thus, if the child is dry at 8:00 A.M. and did not have a BM, you would record the following: "+,++." If the child is wet at 8:30 A.M. but did not have a BM, then you would record the following: "−,++," etc. You should keep two charts on the child — one for "Number of Times" (urinated) and the other for "Number of Times" (BM).

Before using this program, the therapist should make sure that he has a sufficient amount of time to carry out the program in its entirety. The program demands a great deal of therapist involvement and time — as well as consistency.

1. Prepare a Daily Tally Sheet resembling the one presented in Table 4 (Chapter 2). The times listed for each observation should be 10 minutes apart, starting from the time that the child wakes up in the morning to the time that the child goes to bed.
2. The first 7 to 10 days should consist of baseline observation. The therapist should check the child every 10 minutes throughout each day and record when the child is dry/wet or has had/has not had a BM. When the therapist goes to check the child, he/she should say, "Let's

see, [Name], if you are dry." Do not say anything if the child is dry or wet.

At the end of each day, you should record on each chart the respective total number of times that the child wetted or had a BM. To make sure that the baseline period is representative of the child's "normal" toilet habits, be certain that the child is not sick during this period and is eating solids and drinking liquids regularly.

3. At the end of the 7- to 10-day baseline period, review the child's daily tally sheets and determine the time(s) when the child is *most frequently* wet during the day and *most frequently* has a BM. Then, determine the *next most frequent* time(s) that the child wets/has a BM, and so on until you have accounted for 80 percent or more of the times that the child wets or has a BM. For example, you may discover that the child most frequently urinates between 9:30 A.M. and 10:00 A.M. and between 12:00 noon and 12:30 P.M. Similarly, he may most often have a BM between 2:00 P.M. and 3:00 P.M. Next, he may wet frequently between 1:00 P.M. and 1:45 P.M. and between 4:00 P.M. and 5:00 P.M., and has a BM between 10:30 A.M. and 11:00 A.M. and between 6:30 P.M. and 7:00 P.M.

4. After you have determined the "pattern" to the child's toileting habits, you are ready to begin treatment. Continue checking the child every 10 minutes, and again say to him, "Let's see, [Name], if you are dry." But this time, instead of saying nothing *when he is dry*, say the following: "Good boy[girl], you are dry. I am so proud of you. Remember, when you have to go, you should use the potty [toilet]." Then give the child a reward (or token). Make sure he knows that you are pleased with him and that he is thoroughly familiar with the toilet and its location. *If the child is wet* say the following: "No! Bad boy[girl]. You went in your pants. You should go in the potty [toilet], *not* in your pants." Then take the child to the potty (toilet) and say, "This is where you go."

5. When the frequent time periods occur (e.g., between 10:00 and 10:30 A.M.), bring the child to the potty every ten minutes and sit with him for three to five minutes — giving him time to initiate the passage of urine or a BM. If

he goes in the potty—even the slightest amount—express your happiness and joy: kiss him, hug him, pat him on the back, shout "Hurray!" and also reward him with a piece of candy, or other reward. When the child finishes, and when it is appropriate, help him/her wipe himself/herself. Then, have the child pull up his/her underpants and pants (or, pull down her skirt), and repeat the procedure at the next 10-minute period. If the child does not go in the potty, have him/her replace his/her clothing and then return to play or other activity. Check the child again at the next 10-minute period, bring him/her back to the potty, and repeat the same procedure—depending on whether the child goes or does not go in the potty.

When treatment begins you should also make up two new charts to record the child's successes on the potty. The first should state on the vertical line "Number of Times" (urinated in potty), and the second should state "Number of Times" (BM in potty). The horizontal line for both charts should state "Days." Record the child's number of successes on the appropriate chart at the end of each day.

6. As the child's "in potty" successes begin to increase, you should start monitoring him every 20 minutes instead of every 10 minutes. As he approaches 60 percent "in potty" successes, start monitoring him every 40 minutes instead of every 20 minutes. Continue to remind the child that when he has to "go potty" he should proceed by himself and go on the potty—whenever the child goes by himself, he should be praised and rewarded generously.

When the child's "in potty" successes reach 80 percent, you should begin monitoring him every 50 minutes. Continue throughout this period to encourage him to go to the potty by himself whenever he has to go. Praise and reward him whenever he goes by himself. After he reaches 90 percent or above success in the potty, you should monitor him every 60 to 90 minutes. After he reaches 100 percent success, you should monitor him every 90 to 120 minutes and gradually withdraw your monitoring as his 100 percent success rate remains constant over a number of weeks.

Remember to praise the child for any progress in successfully going on the potty. Also, make sure that the child is changed as soon as possible after he has either wet or had a BM in his pants. Change his clothes in a matter-of-fact manner, making sure that you attend to him (and perhaps reward him) as little as possible. *Do not rush the child to become toilet trained.* Many children react in the opposite way when a therapist pushes them to become toilet trained.

Do not continue this program when the child is sick. Many times, a child's sickness will prevent him from controlling his urine and/or bowels. Wait until the child feels better again. If, however, the child indicates to you that he wants to use the potty when he is sick, allow him to do this and reward him for practicing his new toilet habits.

Initially, boys should be allowed to sit while urinating. After they have developed expertise in learning to use the potty, they should then be taught to stand to urinate (and direct their urine stream) and to sit for a BM. Both girls and boys should be taught to wipe themselves well only after they have developed mastery in their new toileting habits.

If the child develops or has enuresis, you should not deal with this problem until he is completely toilet trained. Programs (and devices) which can be used for treating enuresis, as well as alternative programs for toilet training children, are mentioned in Appendix F.

*The success of this program depends on the consistency of the therapist (and his/her assistants or colleagues) throughout the child's day, as well as how the therapist relates to the child.* As the child progresses in his toilet habits and begins to be "dry" for a day or more, you may find that occasional accidents occur. Do not say to the child, "No! Bad boy[girl]. You went in your pants . . . ." Rather, accept the event as an accident and help the child change his clothes. If, however, the accidents become frequent, you may have to begin monitoring the child more often and remind him to use the toilet when he feels he has to pass urine or have a BM. Continue to reward him for using the toilet.

## PROGRAM FOR TEACHING A CHILD TO RECOGNIZE HIS/HER NAME

Throughout the program, praise the child for any progress. Also reward the child at each step with small amounts of his favorite food or drink. Each session should be limited to not more than ten minutes once or twice daily. Since this program makes use of different colors, make sure the child is not partially or totally color blind. You will also need a chart to record the child's progress. The vertical line should state "Number of Steps" and the horizontal line, "Sessions."

1. Write the child's name with red crayon on a piece of white cardboard. Put the name on a table in front of the child and say "[Name], point to your name." You may have to guide the child at first in this activity.
2. Repeat step 1, except this time also place on the table a similar piece of cardboard with another name written on it in a distinctly different color. (This new name should be approximately the same length and size as the child's name, but should not contain any of, or very few of, the same letters.) You may have to guide the child gently at first to help him point to the correct name. Repeat this step until the child can correctly point to his name two consecutive times.
3. Repeat step 2, except reverse the left-right position of the names (that is, if the child's name was originally to the left of the second name, it should now be placed to the right). You may have to guide the child at first before he can correctly choose his name two consecutive times.
4. Repeat steps 2 and 3, alternating the left-right position of his name until he can correctly point to his name two consecutive times. Be sure to praise and reward the child for any progress.
5. Repeat step 4, except replace the second name card with a third card which has the same name written in red. Repeat this step until the child correctly identifies his name two consecutive times. You may have to gently guide the child at first before he can correctly point to his name.

6. Repeat step 5, except replace the third name card with a fourth name card. *The new name should also be written in red, be similar in length, and have few letters in common with the child's name.* Repeat this step until the child is successful two consecutive times. Be sure to alternate the left-right position of the child's name card.

7. Repeat step 6, except alternate the use of the third and fourth names as well as the left-right position of the child's name. Repeat this step until the child can successfully identify his name two consecutive times.

8. This time introduce all three names — each written in red and similar in length. Say to the child, "[Name], point to your name." After each try by the child, change the relative positions of the name cards. Repeat this step until the child correctly identifies his name two consecutive times. (You may have to guide the child at first in correctly choosing his name.)

9. Repeat step 8, except add a fourth name, written in the same color and similar in length to the child's name, but contains many of the letters in the child's name. Again, you may have to guide the child at first in correctly choosing his name. Repeat this step until the child correctly identifies his name two consecutive times.

10. Repeat step 9, except add a fifth name which is also written in red, not the same length as the child's name, and has many letters in common with the child's name. Repeat this step until the child correctly identifies his name two consecutive times.

Remember to praise the child each time he successfully identifies his name. If the child has repeated difficulty proceeding from one particular step to the next, develop an in-between step(s) to help him progress to the next step.

After the child completes step 10, you may want to add and then delete other names of children — again requesting the child to point to his name among those presented to him. You can also vary the color of his name as well as the other names and again ask him to point to his name.

# chapter 7

# Problems and Difficulties in Starting a Behavior Modification Program

*In this chapter, we first discuss program development problems and then present some of the potential difficulties found in carrying out a treatment procedure. Following this discussion, we describe a few methods for helping the child generalize what he has learned to different situations. The chapter ends with a review of the steps in a behavior modification program.*

## Problems in Establishing A Program

After learning about behavior modification procedures, some therapists become confused regarding which behavior they should change first in a child. For example, should they first modify a desirable or undesirable behavior, an especially difficult and complex behavior, or a simple behavior? Although there is no set pattern regarding which type of behavior a therapist should change first, we can suggest a general rule. *Until the therapy agent becomes very familiar with the use of behavior modification procedures, he/she should concentrate on treating rather simple and straightforward behaviors.* Then, as he develops expertise in using these procedures, he can begin tackling more difficult desirable or undesirable behaviors. Some therapists report that they find it easiest first to try out the use of rewards — either strengthening a noncomplex desirable behavior or developing a new self-help skill (e.g., putting on pants) in the child.

Even as a therapist becomes more expert at using these procedures, he should always remember not to expect too much, too fast from a child. Although each of the procedures described in this book has been found to be effective in the treatment of various problems, it takes time for the procedure to have an effect on the child's behavior. How long a period of time is difficult to say. Some children obviously learn faster than others. Some therapists apply procedures better than other therapists. Some environments are more conducive to change in a child than other environments. Each of these factors and others influence how long it will take a procedure to have an effect on a child's behavior.

The only advice that we can offer a therapist is to make sure he has done the best possible job and not necessarily to expect an immediate change in the child's behavior. If, however, a therapist maintains that he has tried to apply a procedure as well as possible and has not found any change in the child's behavior after a significant amount of time, he should consider changing or revising the procedure.

Before changing the procedure, however, the therapist should be sure that the child knows what is expected of him. For example, if we are interested in developing eye contact in a nonverbal child, he can learn what is expected of him through the therapist's use of a prompting procedure. Similarly, a therapist could also use prompting to teach a nonverbal child to cooperatively play and interact with other children, to sit in a chair, to attend to an educational task, and so forth. A verbal child, on the other hand, could be told what the therapist expects of him, or the behavior could be demonstrated for him.

In establishing a program, a therapy agent should also be certain that each of the therapists and therapy assistants is thoroughly familiar with the treatment procedure and is willing to carry out the procedure. Too often a therapist spends a great deal of time and effort in setting up a treatment procedure without ever informing the other therapists and assistants about the program or obtaining their agreement to participate in it. *If the other people who work with the child do not participate in the treatment program, this will likely decrease the overall effectiveness of the program.* The degree to which the program is affected will be determined largely by the target behavior being changed and the situation in which it is changed. If, for example, a child is being taught to eat with a spoon at breakfast by Mrs. Jones, and this is not followed through at lunch and dinner by Mrs. Thomas and Mr. Smith (the child being permitted to eat with his hands), it will be more difficult for the child to master independent eating with a spoon. Similarly, if time out is used by one therapist to reduce tantrums in the classroom and the other therapist prefers to use attention to the tantrums to "help" the child, his tantrums are not likely to decrease. On the other hand, if a therapist plans to teach a child a behavior (or reduce a behavior) only in a situation in which the therapist has complete control, then the program is likely to be more successful — although the modified behavior probably will not generalize to any other situation.

Related to the problem of therapist involvement is the issue of therapist motivation in the change procedure. Therapists differ in motivation to work with a child. Whenever possible, each therapist involved in a treatment program should have a comparable motivational interest in treating the child and a willingness to contribute the necessary time (and make the necessary sacrifices) to maximize the potential effectiveness of the program.

Before finalizing any treatment program, a therapist should be sure that he is comfortable with the use of the procedure being suggested. This is especially true for those procedures described in Chapter 5. Some procedures for reducing behavior may be more acceptable to the therapist than others, and he should be aware of which ones these are. Even under ideal circumstances, a treatment procedure is not likely to be effective if the therapist does not feel at ease and sure of himself with it.

## Difficulties in Carrying Out The Program

Sometimes after a program has been started a therapist notices that the child is refusing to participate — showing, for example, negativism or boredom. This can be caused by many factors. The reward being used may no longer be attractive to the child; he may view the whole situation as aversive because of various procedures to which he has been exposed; the amount of reward he is receiving for each desirable behavior may be too little; the child may perceive the therapist as disinterested in him and his progress; the program is perhaps being used incorrectly; and so forth.

If there is a problem with the reward, check the following: the quality, amount, type, and schedule of reward the child is receiving; the immediacy with which the reward is being given and the type of social (verbal) reward the child is receiving; and the appropriateness of the use of token versus tangible rewards (token reward systems do not necessarily work with nonverbal, isolate children but may be effective with children who are more socially interactive and verbal). The problem could also be related to how the procedure is being applied. Review the procedure a second time to be sure it is being used correctly and consistently. Inconsistency, as we have mentioned a number of times, can be a major cause of problems in the use of a treatment procedure.

The child's negative behavior may also be an attempt by him to take control of the situation. If this appears to be the case, the therapist should place this behavior on extinction, ignoring the child during this period and generously rewarding him when he is ready to begin treatment again. The therapist should, however, make sure that this does not become a "game" for the child. If the negativism continues, the therapist should consider using a different procedure.

Another problem which occasionally develops is related to the use of the extinction procedure. Some researchers have recently noted that in some cases in which adult attention is withdrawn following the occurrence of a child's undesirable behavior, the behavior not only initially increases but also stays at a high level — even after as long as two weeks. Although we should theoretically expect the behavior to decrease (assuming, of course, that the attention was rewarding the behavior), it is inappropriate to suggest that the therapist allow this behavior to continue for such a long period of time. Thus, if a therapist chooses to use extinction, he should monitor its effectiveness closely, and if he does not observe a decrease in the child's behavior within relatively few sessions, he should discontinue the procedure and establish a new program (e.g., developing an incompatible desirable behavior or time out).

This is another reason why it is so important to chart a child's progress. Charting is the only way we can monitor the child's day-to-day, session-to-session progress and thereby know whether to intervene in the treatment program. It is also important to continue charting the child's target behavior (though not as often) after treatment has stopped. By doing this *follow-up* work, the therapist is able to know in a relatively short period of time whether or not a reintroduction of the treatment program is necessary.

One additional difficulty which sometimes arises in the carrying out of a behavior modification program is not related to the treatement procedure or to the child; rather, the difficulty is with the therapist. We have already discussed therapist expectations and involvement as potential problems. The other area of difficulty is related to the therapist's concern about the lack of equal or sufficient time to interact with the other children for whom he is responsible. This is an especially difficult problem, since the other children may feel that they have the "right" to equal time. They may also become jealous of the child with whom the therapist is working and express this jealousy in an aggressive manner (not necessarily toward the target child).

The therapist should be sensitive to this potential problem and spend as much of his available time with the other children as possible. He should also explain to the children what he is doing and why it is being done. In some cases, in fact, the therapist can also solicit the help of the other children. This will have two effects: (1) it will bring the "outsiders" inside and make them feel that they are part of the same situation with the therapist—not apart from the therapist, and (2) the therapist will have additional help in maintaining consistency in the treatment of the child. The therapist can also solicit the assistance of other adults. Most parents, teachers, nurses, attendants, and clinicians who are near a college or university will find many students who are quite willing to volunteer their help. A phone call to, for example, a professor or the campus student services center can start the process. Assistance can also be obtained from mature, responsible students from a local high school. By enlisting the aid of others, the therapist will find that he will have more time than he originally thought to spend with the other children (as well as have time for outside social activities).

## Generalization of The Child's Behavior

When we modify a child's behavior, we typically do it in a particular situation or within a limited number of situations. Since these situations are associated with learning what to do (or what not to do), we find that the child tends to perform the learned behavior only when these situations occur. In other words, *these situations have situational control of the child's behavior*. This means, for example, that a child once toilet trained at school may not be toilet trained at home. Similarly, a child who learns that he can throw a tantrum at home to obtain what he wants may not do this at school because the situation is different.

Some time ago, a psychologist helped a teacher control a child's frequent hitting of other children using a time out procedure for the undesirable behavior and reward for desirable behaviors. The child's behavior was reduced to an occasional weekly hit within a three-week period. The parents happened to come to school shortly after this period to observe their child and were amazed to discover that their daughter was not hitting other children. They reported that they were having repeated difficulty controlling her hitting of neighborhood children. Thus, it appears that the child's decreased hitting of other children in school did not generalize to another situation.

Thus, in order for treatment to be completely effective, we must teach the child to generalize the learned behavior to other situations. But how? The question is not an easy one to answer, but we can provide the therapist with some guidelines regarding maximizing generalization (it should be pointed out in advance that none of the following statements are necessarily mutually exclusive).

1. As therapy progresses and the child's behavior noticeably changes, begin gradually to bring into the treatment situation other people with whom the child interacts. At first, these people should just observe. Eventually, they should take an active role in treatment—making sure that they use the same instructions, commands, and so forth as the therapist and carry out the treatment procedure in the *same way* as the therapist. These people should then be encouraged to use the same approach with the child in those situations in which they interact with the child.

2. As the child's behavior noticeably changes and starts to stabilize at an acceptable (but not necessarily final) level, the therapist should bring the child into other situations and apply the treatment procedure. As the child's behavior changes in these situations also, the therapist should bring in those people with whom the child interacts in these new situ-

ations. They should then be trained to apply the same procedure as the therapist.

3. If a child shows the same target behavior in more than one situation (e.g., at home, at school, and with a babysitter), before treatment begins all the people involved in these situations should meet and agree on *one* treatment approach. Each person should then apply the procedure. Regular meetings should be held among these people to discuss the child's progress as well as any problems.

Obviously, one cannot expose the child to every conceivable set of circumstances in which the target behavior might occur, but by exposing the child to as many different situations as possible, the therapist will maximize the generalization of the learned behavior.

## Review of Steps in A Behavior Modification Program

1. Identify the target behavior to be modified. The behavior must be objective.
2. Choose a plan for observing the target behavior.
3. Prepare a progress chart for the child.
4. Establish a criterion for the successful treatment of the target behavior.
5. Describe what will specifically occur when the child performs the desirable behavior. Or, describe what will specifically occur to teach the child the desirable behavior.
6. Describe what will specifically occur when the child performs the undesirable behavior. Or, describe what will specifically occur to teach the child to reduce the undesirable behavior.
7. Decide on the extent of the baseline period. Describe what the therapist will specifically do during baseline.
8. Initiate the baseline phase. Chart the child's target behavior.
9. Initiate the treatment procedure. Continue charting.
10. Monitor the effectiveness of the procedure; make changes in the procedure as appropriate.
11. Do a follow-up.

## Study Questions

1. In choosing a target behavior, what is the best strategy for a therapy agent who is using behavior modification procedures for the first time?

(Review p. 169 to check your answer.)

2. What should a therapist expect regarding the effectiveness of a behavior modification procedure?

(Review pp. 169–170 to check your answer.)

3. Why should different people who work with a child be involved in his treatment?

(Review pp. 170–171 to check your answer.)

4. List four factors which can contribute to a child's refusal to participate in a therapy program.
    a.
    b.
    c.
    d.
(Review pp. 171–172 to check your answer.)

5. What problems are associated with the use of the extinction procedure, and why is charting important when this procedure is used?

(Review p. 172 to check your answer.)

6. Why should a therapist do a follow-up?

(Review p. 172 to check your answer.)

7. List three potential therapist problems in the use of behavior modification procedures.
   a.
   b.
   c.
   (Review pp. 171–173 to check your answer.)

8. List three methods of assisting a child in generalizing his learned behavior.
   a.
   b.
   c.
   (Review pp. 174–175 to check your answer.)

9. Review the steps in a behavior modification program and then apply them to the treatment of a particular child.

*appendix* **A**

# Behavior Evaluation
# Checklist

# BEHAVIOR EVALUATION CHECKLIST[10]

Child's name:_____

Child's address:_____ Evaluation date:_____

Name of person performing evaluation:_____

## MOTOR SKILLS CHECKLIST

| | | Always | Sometimes | Never | Comments |
|---|---|---|---|---|---|
| A. | Grasps objects | | | | |
| | Sits unaided | | | | |
| | Creeps | | | | |
| | Walks with assistance | | | | |
| | Toddles | | | | |
| | Walks without assistance | | | | |
| | Runs | | | | |
| | Jumps | | | | |
| | Climbs stairs with assistance | | | | |
| | Climbs stairs without assistance | | | | |
| | Ascends stairs alternating feet | | | | |
| | Descends stairs alternating feet | | | | |
| | Marches | | | | |
| | Hops | | | | |
| | Bounces ball | | | | |
| | Throws ball without direction | | | | |
| | Throws ball with direction | | | | |
| | Catches ball | | | | |
| | Kicks ball | | | | |
| | Rides a bicycle | | | | |
| | Skips alternating feet | | | | |
| | | | | | |
| B. | Touches toes without bending knees | | | | |
| | Can perform sit-up | | | | |
| | Performs 5 knee bends or more | | | | |
| | Performs 3 push-ups | | | | |
| | Performs 5 sit-ups | | | | |
| | Performs broad jump of 2' or more | | | | |
| | Can chin self twice or more | | | | |

## SELF-CARE SKILLS CHECKLIST

| | Always | Sometimes | Never | Comments |
|---|---|---|---|---|
| Indicates bathroom need | | | | |
| Dresses self after toileting | | | | |
| Uses toilet paper | | | | |
| Flushes toilet | | | | |

[10]This checklist is from an evaluation form used and developed by the Syracuse Developmental Center, Syracuse, New York; reproduced with permission.

## SELF-CARE SKILLS CHECKLIST

| | Always | Sometimes | Never | Comments |
|---|---|---|---|---|
| Washes hands | | | | |
| Can blow nose | | | | |
| Uses tissue or handkerchief | | | | |
| Can drink from a glass | | | | |
| Can use a straw | | | | |
| Can button clothing | | | | |
| Can zip clothing | | | | |
| Can snap clothing | | | | |
| Can undress self | | | | |
| Can put socks on | | | | |
| Can tie shoes | | | | |
| Can put coat or sweater on | | | | |
| Can put pants or skirt on | | | | |
| Can put shirt or blouse on | | | | |
| Can put dress on | | | | |
| Can use a spoon | | | | |
| Can use a fork | | | | |
| Can use a knife | | | | |
| Can eat a sandwich | | | | |
| Can drink from soda bottle or can | | | | |
| Closes mouth when eating | | | | |
| Is tidy when eating | | | | |
| Cleans up after eating | | | | |

## COMMAND FOLLOWING CHECKLIST

| | | | | |
|---|---|---|---|---|
| Attention Toward Therapist | | | | |
| Makes eye contact (for 1–3 sec.) on command with prompt | | | | |
| Makes eye contact (for more than 3 sec.) on command with prompt | | | | |
| Makes eye contact (for 1–3 sec.) on command | | | | |
| Makes eye contact (for more than 3 sec.) on command | | | | |
| Attention Toward Other Children | | | | |
| Looks at other children on command with prompt (for 1–3 sec.) | | | | |
| Looks at other children on command with prompt (for more than 3 sec.) | | | | |

## COMMAND FOLLOWING CHECKLIST

| | Always | Sometimes | Never | Comments |
|---|---|---|---|---|
| Looks at other children on command (for 1—3 sec.) | | | | |
| Looks at other children on command (for more than 3 sec.) | | | | |
| General Command Following | | | | |
| Grasps particular object on command | | | | |
| Gives an object to adult on command | | | | |
| Gives an object to another child on command | | | | |
| Picks up object from toy box on command | | | | |
| Places object in toy box on command | | | | |
| Touches another child on command | | | | |
| Responds to the command "Come to me" | | | | |
| Responds to the command "Sit down" | | | | |
| Responds to the command "Put that down" | | | | |
| Imitates one simple motor behavior on command | | | | |
| Imitates two simple motor behaviors on command | | | | |
| Imitates 3—5 simple motor behaviors on command | | | | |
| Imitates 5—10 simple motor behaviors on command | | | | |
| Imitates 10 or more simple motor behaviors on command | | | | |
| Imitates speech sounds on command | | | | |
| Imitates words on command | | | | |
| Imitates simple sentences on command | | | | |
| Imitates a two—stage motor behavior sequence on command | | | | |
| Imitates a three—stage motor behavior sequence on command | | | | |
| Imitates a 4— or 5— stage motor behavior sequence on command | | | | |

## COMMUNICATION SKILLS CHECKLIST

| | Always | Sometimes | Never | Comments |
|---|---|---|---|---|
| Expresses self by facial gestures | | | | |
| Expresses self by manual gestures | | | | |
| Produces undifferentiated sounds | | | | |

## COMMUNICATION SKILLS CHECKLIST

| | Always | Sometimes | Never | Comments |
|---|---|---|---|---|
| Produces vowel sounds | | | | |
| Produces consonant sounds | | | | |
| Can say single words | | | | |
| Can say phrases | | | | |
| Says simple sentences | | | | |
| Responds to name | | | | |
| Listens to stories | | | | |
| Can repeat a story | | | | |
| Identifies objects by matching | | | | |
| Identifies objects by pointing | | | | |
| Identifies objects by name | | | | |
| Identifies parts of the body by pointing | | | | |
| Verbally identifies parts of the body | | | | |
| Greets people | | | | |
| Delivers message orally | | | | |
| Traces printed letters | | | | |
| Copies printed letters | | | | |
| Copies printed numbers | | | | |
| Prints unaided | | | | |
| Produces cursive writing | | | | |
| Writes first name | | | | |
| Writes last name | | | | |
| Writes full name | | | | |
| Can verbally spell name | | | | |
| Reads on a primer level | | | | |
| Reads on 1st-grade level | | | | |
| Reads on 2nd-grade level | | | | |

## MANIPULATIVE SKILLS CHECKLIST

| | Always | Sometimes | Never | Comments |
|---|---|---|---|---|
| Can trace a line | | | | |
| Can draw a straight line | | | | |
| Can join a series of dots | | | | |
| Produces vertical lines | | | | |
| Produces horizontal lines | | | | |
| Produces curved lines | | | | |
| Produces diagonal lines | | | | |
| Reproduces a square from a model | | | | |

**184**

## MANIPULATIVE SKILLS CHECKLIST

| | Always | Sometimes | Never | Comments |
|---|---|---|---|---|
| Reproduces a circle from a model | | | | |
| Reproduces a triangle from a model | | | | |
| Can string large beads | | | | |
| Can string medium beads | | | | |
| Can string small beads | | | | |
| Can fold paper | | | | |
| Can fold paper in half | | | | |
| Can fold paper in quarters | | | | |
| Can roll clay | | | | |
| Can cut with scissors | | | | |
| Can cut on a line with scissors | | | | |
| Smears finger paints | | | | |
| Creates images with finger paints | | | | |
| Uses a paint brush | | | | |
| Uses a peg board | | | | |
| Can paste | | | | |
| Handles building blocks | | | | |
| Holds crayon | | | | |
| Scribbles | | | | |
| Colors within a designated area | | | | |
| Draws face with eyes, mouth and nose | | | | |
| Draws face with above features plus hair and ears | | | | |
| Draws variety of facial expressions | | | | |

## ACADEMIC SKILLS CHECKLIST

| | Always | Sometimes | Never | Comments |
|---|---|---|---|---|
| Discrimination | | | | |
| Differentiates between very different objects (e.g., table and chair) | | | | |
| Differentiates between similar objects (e.g., pants and skirt) | | | | |
| Differentiates between very different sounds (e.g., talking and object dropping) | | | | |
| Differentiates between similar sounds (e.g., knocking on wood and metal) | | | | |
| Number Concepts | | | | |
| Matches numerals 1—9 | | | | |
| Matches numerals 10—20 | | | | |
| Counts aloud 1—9 | | | | |

**185**

## ACADEMIC SKILLS CHECKLIST

| | Always | Sometimes | Never | Comments |
|---|---|---|---|---|
| Counts aloud 10-19 | | | | |
| Reads numerals 1-9 | | | | |
| Reads numerals 10-19 | | | | |
| Reads numerals 20-50 | | | | |
| Reads numerals over 100 | | | | |
| Identifies numerals out of sequence | | | | |
| Time Concept | | | | |
| Can recognize small and large hands on clock | | | | |
| States where the hands of clock are (e.g., little hand on 10, big hand on 3) | | | | |
| Tells time to the hour | | | | |
| Tells time to the half-hour | | | | |
| Tells time to the quarter-hour | | | | |
| Tells time to the minute | | | | |
| Addition | | | | |
| Adds 1 to any number under 5 | | | | |
| Adds 1 to any number under 10 | | | | |
| Adds 2 to any number under 5 | | | | |
| Adds 2 to any number under 10 | | | | |
| Adds combination of numbers totaling to 9 | | | | |
| Adds combination of numbers totaling to 20 | | | | |
| Performs addition to 20, mentally without physical aides | | | | |
| Subtraction | | | | |
| Subtracts 1 from any number under 5 | | | | |
| Subtracts 1 from any number under 10 | | | | |
| Subtracts 2 from any number under 5 | | | | |
| Subtracts 2 from any number under 10 | | | | |
| Can subtract any number less than 10 from 10 | | | | |
| Can subtract any number less than 20 from 20 | | | | |
| Money Concepts | | | | |
| Recognizes "real" money | | | | |
| Selects specific coin on request | | | | |
| Arranges coins in order by value | | | | |

## ACADEMIC SKILLS CHECKLIST

| | Always | Sometimes | Never | Comments |
|---|---|---|---|---|
| Makes change for quarter | | | | |
| Makes change for dollar | | | | |

## SOCIAL SKILLS CHECKLIST

| | Always | Sometimes | Never | Comments |
|---|---|---|---|---|
| Can communicate positive feelings | | | | |
| Can communicate anger | | | | |
| Can communicate sadness | | | | |
| Controls temper | | | | |
| Is aware of others | | | | |
| Is courteous | | | | |
| Does what he is asked | | | | |
| Is truthful | | | | |
| Is dependable | | | | |
| Is accepted by peers | | | | |
| Accepts help from adults | | | | |
| Accepts help from peers | | | | |
| Recognizes ownership of objects | | | | |
| Respects property of others | | | | |
| Waits turn | | | | |
| Shares with others | | | | |
| Adapts to change in routine | | | | |
| Displays good sportsmanship | | | | |
| Shows leadership | | | | |
| Responds well to kindness | | | | |
| Shows affection to others | | | | |
| Offers assistance to peers | | | | |
| Offers assistance to less able residents | | | | |
| Can be taken on field trips | | | | |

## MISCELLANEOUS SKILLS CHECKLIST

| | Always | Sometimes | Never | Comments |
|---|---|---|---|---|
| Likes to watch T.V. | | | | |
| Likes to listen to music | | | | |
| Likes to listen to stories | | | | |
| Likes to be held | | | | |
| Likes to sing | | | | |
| Likes to talk | | | | |
| Likes physical activity | | | | |
| Likes to be read to | | | | |
| Likes to read | | | | |

## MISCELLANEOUS SKILLS CHECKLIST

| | Always | Sometimes | Never | Comments |
|---|---|---|---|---|
| Likes to eat meals | | | | |
| Likes candy snacks | | | | |
| Likes to be alone | | | | |
| Likes to be with peers | | | | |
| Likes to be with staff | | | | |
| Likes to sleep | | | | |
| Likes group activites | | | | |

*appendix* **B**

# Record Sheets

Child's name:_____
Child's behavior
being worked with:_____
Your name:_____
Date:_____

BEHAVIOR TALLY SHEET

Total number of times behavior
occurred per hour, day, session, etc.

_____

Therapist's name:_____
Week of:_____
Child's name:_____
Child's behavior
being worked with:_____

BEHAVIOR TALLY SHEET

Day of
Week

_____

_____

_____

_____

_____

Therapist's name: _____
Week of: _____
Child's name: _____
Child's behavior
being worked with: _____

## BEHAVIOR TALLY SHEET

Day of
Week    min.              Hour

|  | 15 |  |  |  |  |  |  |
|---|---|---|---|---|---|---|---|
|  | 30 |  |  |  |  |  |  |
|  | 45 |  |  |  |  |  |  |
|  | 60 |  |  |  |  |  |  |

Average ____ ____ ____ ____ ____ ____ ____ ____

|  | 15 |  |  |  |  |  |  |
|---|---|---|---|---|---|---|---|
|  | 30 |  |  |  |  |  |  |
|  | 45 |  |  |  |  |  |  |
|  | 60 |  |  |  |  |  |  |

Average ____ ____ ____ ____ ____ ____ ____ ____

|  | 15 |  |  |  |  |  |  |
|---|---|---|---|---|---|---|---|
|  | 30 |  |  |  |  |  |  |
|  | 45 |  |  |  |  |  |  |
|  | 60 |  |  |  |  |  |  |

Average ____ ____ ____ ____ ____ ____ ____ ____

|  | 15 |  |  |  |  |  |  |
|---|---|---|---|---|---|---|---|
|  | 30 |  |  |  |  |  |  |
|  | 45 |  |  |  |  |  |  |
|  | 60 |  |  |  |  |  |  |

Average ____ ____ ____ ____ ____ ____ ____ ____

|  | 15 |  |  |  |  |  |  |
|---|---|---|---|---|---|---|---|
|  | 30 |  |  |  |  |  |  |
|  | 45 |  |  |  |  |  |  |
|  | 60 |  |  |  |  |  |  |

Average ____ ____ ____ ____ ____ ____ ____ ____

*appendix* C

# Behavior Chart

Use back side for comments
on child's performance

Child's name: _____
Target behavior: _____
Date: _____
Therapist's initials: _____

Number
of times

Percent
of times

Number of
minutes

Number of
steps

(Circle one)

0  1  2  3  4  5  6  7  8  9  10  11  12  13  14  15  16  17  18  19  20

Days, Sessions, Hours, or Weeks (Circle one)

**197**

*appendix* **D**

# Possible Rewards to Use in Behavior Modification With Children

## Possible Rewards To Use in Behavior Modification With Children[11]

A. Edibles

*Snacks and sweets (given in small pieces when necessary):*
Pretzels
Cookies (e.g., Animal Crackers or other small cookies)
Sugared cereals (e.g., Sugar Loops, Cap'n Krunch)
Candy (e.g., M&Ms, jelly beans, chocolate chips)
Ice cream (spoonful from a cup)
Cake (e.g., Twinkies, cupcakes)
Raisins
Peanuts
Pudding
Gelatin
Marshmallows
French fried potatoes
Potato chips (including corn chips, etc.)
Fruit (including cherries, grapes, oranges, etc.)
Pies

B. Liquids

*Drinks typically given in small sips*:
Carbonated (e.g., cola)
Noncarbonated (e.g., orange drink, grape drink, Kool-Aid)
Juices
Milk

C. Objects

*Relating to personal hygiene*:

| | | |
|---|---|---|
| Hairbrush | Soap | Deodorant |
| Toothpaste | Mouthwash | Makeup |
| Toothbrush | Perfume | Hair tonic |

---

[11]Based on Larsen, L. A., & Bricker, W. A. *A manual for parents and teachers of severely and profoundly retarded children.* Nashville, Tenn.: IMRID Papers and Reports, vol. V, no. 22, 1968. Reprinted by permission of the authors and of the John F. Kennedy Center for Research on Education and Human Development, George Peabody College for Teachers.

*Jewelery and clothing*:

| | |
|---|---|
| Bracelet | Football helmet |
| Watch | Sweatshirt |
| Ring | Blouse |
| Necklace | Skirt |
| Ribbon | Pants |
| Barrette | Belt |
| Key chain | Socks |
| Wallet | Shoes |
| Purse | Underwear |
| Bathing suit | Decals |
| Hat | Gym shoes (sneakers) |

*Toys and games*:

| | |
|---|---|
| Speedster cars | Trucks |
| Dolls | Waterguns |
| Mechanical toys | Sand and pail and shovel |
| Whistles | Bubble blower |
| Balloons | Puzzles |
| Tops | |

*Miscellaneous*:
Pen (with paper)
Pencil (with paper)
Chalk with slate
Reading material (comic books, children's stories)
Building blocks
Crayons and coloring paper
Clay

D.  Activities

*Outdoor activities*:
Playing catch with therapist
Playing on swings
Playing on jungle gym
Going on merry-go-round
Bicycle ride
Running
Playing tag or hide-and-go-seek with therapist
Going for a walk with therapist
Playing with a pet (dog, kitten, gerbil, etc.)
Playing catch

Going on the teeter-totter
Jumping rope with the therapist

*Indoor activities*:
Playing catch, playing with a ball
Watching a cartoon on film or on television
Watching a television program
Looking through a book or magazine
Jumping rope with the therapist
Playing in the gym (unstructured play)
Playing "chase"
Hearing music from phonograph/radio
Riding on rocking horse
Running
Finger painting with the therapist

*Special activities*:
Home visit
Trip to the museum
Trip to the zoo
Trip to the beach, swimming pool
Automobile ride
Trip to the therapist's home
Trip to the circus or carnival
A hike

E. Social Praise

*Expressions*:
"Good," "Good boy [girl]"
"Very good."
"I like that."
"That's good."
"I'm glad you did that."
"I appreciate what you have done."
"That's right."
"That's it . . . very good."
"You did a good job."
"Mmm-hmm."
"Fine."
"You did it. Very good."
"Thank you," "Thank you very much."
"I'm so happy [pleased] with you," "I'm proud of you."

F. Nonverbal Messages and Movements

*Facial expressions*:
Smiling
Expression of surprise and delight
Nodding head in an approving manner
Laughing
Winking

*Proximity to child*:
Standing near child
Sitting near child

*Physical contact with child*:
Hugging
Patting back/head/arm; ruffling hair
Touching arm
Rubbing back
Kissing
Picking child up and holding him/her
Wrestling
Tickling
Bouncing child on knees
Playing patty-cake

*appendix* **E**

# Selected Films
# on Behavior Modification
# With Children

# Selected Films on Behavior Modification With Children[12]

*Each of the films listed may be rented or purchased from the distributor whose address accompanies each listing. The rental fee varies from free to about $60. Most of the films can be kept from one to three days.*

*The ABC's of behavior modification* (1972, 20 minutes, color, 16mm., sound, $20.00 daily rental, $175.00 purchase)

> Educational Division
> Hallmark Films, Inc.
> 1511 East North Avenue
> Baltimore, Maryland 21213

This film emphasizes the relationships between *A*ntecedents, *B*ehaviors, and *C*onsequences and describes how antecedents and consequents can be programmed in a school environment to influence staff and students. The students in this film are from 12 to 17 years of age and are being taught in the Anne Arundel County (Maryland) Learning Center. The students have a variety of academic and social deficits. Motivation is built through the use of positive reinforcement.

*Achievement place* (1970, 30 minutes, black-and-white, 16mm., sound, $7.00 daily rental, $11.20 weekly rental)

> University of Kansas
> Bureau of Visual Instruction
> 6 Bailey Hall
> Lawrence, Kansas 66044

This is a documentary on the day-to-day activities at Achievement Place, a foster home for predelinquent boys. The home is located in Lawrence, Kansas, and is operated within an operant conditioning framework.

*Ask just for little things* (n.d., 20 minutes, color, 16mm., sound, $25.00 daily rental, $250.00 purchase)

---

[12]The author wishes to express his gratitude to those distributors who provided descriptive material and information regarding their films. Information on some of the films was obtained from *Filmography,* prepared by Rosemary O. Nelson and distributed at the Eighth Annual Convention of the Association for Advancement of Behavior Therapy, November 1974, Chicago, Illinois.

Educational Division
Hallmark Films, Inc.
1511 East North Avenue
Baltimore, Maryland 21213

This film follows the *Genesis* film (described on p. 209) in the Step Behind Series. Whereas *Genesis* concentrates on teaching self-help skills to the retarded, this film concentrates on teaching life skills. In particular three life skills are taught: ambulation, personal hygiene, and attending. These skills will provide the retarded child with a larger repertoire of behaviors to help him function more fully in our everyday society.

*Behavior modification: Teaching language to psychotic children* (1969, 42 minutes, color, 16mm., sound, $42.20 daily rental, $500.90 purchase)

Prentice-Hall, Inc.
Film Library
Englewood Cliffs, New Jersey 07632

This film, based on the work of Ivar Lovaas at UCLA, demonstrates the use of behavior modification techniques to teach language skills to psychotic children. Frequent use of graphs and charts illustrates the effects of the treatment procedure. The opening scenes portray psychotic behavior prior to treatment. This behavior lessens as therapy progresses.

*Behavior therapy with an autistic child* (1964, 42 minutes, black-and-white, 16 mm., sound, free rental)

U. S. Public Health Service
Audio-Visual Service
Washington, D.C. 20014

This film demonstrates the use of operant conditioning techniques in helping an autistic child learn to perform simple motor tasks. An introduction is given by Leonard Krasner and Gerald Davison.

*The broken bridge* (n.d., 35 minutes, color, 16mm., $40.00 rental, $400.00 purchase)

Multi-Media Division
Time-Life Films
43 West 16th Street
New York, New York 10011

Therapy sessions with autistic children are shown. The therapist is

Irene Kassorla, and she demonstrates how to establish communication skills in autistic children. Three steps are shown: imitation learning; responses to questions; and initiative question asking.

*Genesis* (1971, 25 minutes, color, 16mm., sound, $25.00 daily rental, $250.00 purchase)

> Educational Division
> Hallmark Films, Inc.
> 1511 East North Avenue
> Baltimore, Maryland 21213

This is the first film in the Step Behind Series. The film teaches how to train basic self-help skills like dressing, eating, and toileting in mentally retarded persons. Step-by-step procedures are detailed. The techniques demonstrated in this film are based on well-established principles of learning.

*Help for Mark* (1970, 17 minutes, color, 16mm., sound, $19.00 rental, $210.90 purchase)

> Prentice-Hall, Inc.
> Film Library
> Englewood Cliffs, New Jersey 07632

This film gives the most attention to the use of behavior modification procedures and techniques with retarded children which can be used in the home environment. Careful comparison of behavior exhibited before, during, and after training reveals the need for keeping accurate records of the child's progress. Problems, such as those arising from reinforcement of undesirable behavior, are discussed in detail.

*Horizon of hope* (n.d., 15 minutes, color, $13.00 rental, $180.00 purchase)

> Extension Media Center
> University of California
> Berkeley, California 94720

The use of reinforcement with learning-disabled children is demonstrated at a special school at the UCLA Neuropsychiatric Institute. Although the disabilities have various causes, reinforcement can still be shown to be helpful in teaching appropriate behaviors to these children.

*I'll promise you a tomorrow* (n.d., 20 minutes, color, 16mm., sound, $25.00 daily rental, $250.00 purchase)

Educational Division
Hallmark Films, Inc.
1511 East North Avenue
Baltimore, Maryland 21213

This is the final film in the Step Behind Series (the others are *Genesis* and *Ask just for little things*). After the child is taught self-help skills and life skills, the next area of concern is teaching him more advanced skills to prepare him for a special education setting. In particular, communication, direction following, and group participation are illustrated in this film.

*An individual behavior modification program* (n.d., 14 minutes, color, 16mm., $25.00 rental, $225.00 purchase)

Dr. Jacqueline Montgomery
Box A
Camarillo State Hospital
Camarillo, California 93010

This film introduces behavior modification procedures on a basic level of understanding. Steps in the development of a behavior modification program are detailed, illustrating the importance of specifying the behavior to be changed, taking baselines, charting, and implementing a consistent treatment program.

*Operant conditioning—token economy* (n.d., 40 minutes, color, 16 mm., $40.00 rental, $350.00 purchase)

Dr. Jacqueline Montgomery
Box A
Camarillo State Hospital
Camarillo, California 93010

This film demonstrates the use of operant conditioning procedures, particularly positive reinforcement and token economy systems. The film depicts a day in the life of a mentally retarded resident on a token economy system.

*Out of the shadows* (n.d., 17 minutes, color, 16mm., $10.00 rental, $120.00 purchase)

Audio-Visual Center
6 Bailey Hall
University of Kansas
Lawrence, Kansas 66044

This film demonstrates the use of behavior modification procedures to help retarded children learn basic self-help and social skills (e.g., feeding, motor skills, speech, toileting). Emphasis is placed on the use of reinforcement methods.

*Pinpoint, record and consequate* (1967, 14 minutes, color, 16mm., sound, $25.00 five-day rental, $260.00 purchase)
>Film Fund
>Box 3026
>Kansas City, Kansas 66103

Precision teaching—adapting operant conditioning principles to home behavior management—is demonstrated. The three steps in this procedure (Pinpoint, Record, and Consequate) are described, and graphs are shown of how parents use this procedure.

*PREP (Preparation through responsive educational programs)* (n.d., 27 minutes, color, 16mm., $25.00 rental, purchase price not available)
>Communication Resource Center
>Institute for Behavioral Research
>2429 Linden Lane
>Silver Spring, Maryland 20910

Remedial educational procedures are shown with adolescent youth who have social and/or academic problems. Emphasis is on the use of an elaborate reinforcement system. Interpersonal skills training is also shown, as well as parent training and follow-up evaluation.

*Reward procedures for behavior management* (1971, 25 minutes, black-and-white, 16mm., $21.00 two-day rental, $175.00 purchase)
>Behavior Technics, Inc.
>Box 116
>Lemont, Pennsylvania 16851

This film offers the observer a basic introduction to the topic of child management through reinforcement methods. It presents three simple reinforcement procedures that adults can use to influence child behavior.

*Rewards and reinforcements in learning* (1969, 26 minutes, black-and-white, 16mm., sound, $20.00 three-day rental, $190.00 purchase)
>Behavior Modification Productions
>Box 3207
>Scottsdale, Arizona 85257

This film shows the use of operant conditioning procedures with both normal and retarded children of both preschool and school age. Emphasis is on modifying rather complex human behaviors and showing the progress of the children over time. The film also demonstrates how behavior modification procedures can be applied to disadvantaged children in the classroom. The narration provides the observer with additional information on the application of these procedures. An excellent study guide is also available for a modest fee.

*Self-management of behavior* (n.d., 33 minutes, color, 16mm., sound, $50.00 normal rental, $300.00 two-year rental)

> Mental Retardation Program Media Unit
> Neuropsychiatric Institute
> UCLA Center for the Health Sciences
> 760 Westwood Plaza
> Los Angeles, California 90024

The development of self-regulatory behavior (managing one's own behavior) is demonstrated with two children through the use of behavior modification procedures. B.F. Skinner narrates.

*Teaching language skills to children with behavioral disorders* (1972, 40 minutes, black-and-white, 16mm., sound, $25,00 rental, $185.00 purchase, $85.00 videotape purchase)

> Behavior Modification Technology
> P.O. Box 597
> Libertyville, Illinois 60048

This film demonstrates a program for teaching receptive language and speech. The use of reinforcement, fading, shaping, prompting, and chaining is shown. It is designed to be used in conjunction with *Teaching self-help skills to children with behavioral disorders*.

*Teaching self-help skills to children with behavioral disorders* (1972, 40 minutes, black-and-white, 16mm., sound, $25.00 rental, $185.00 purchase, $85.00 videotape purchase)

> Behavior Modification Technology
> P.O. Box 597
> Libertyville, Illinois 60048

Behavior modification programs are detailed for teaching various self-help skills to retarded children and other children with behavior disorders. The film shows the use of reinforcement, shaping, stimulus control, prompting and other behavior modification procedures.

*Teaching social recreational skills to children with behavioral disorders* (1972, 40 minutes, black-and-white, 16mm., sound, $25.00 rental, $185.00 purchase, $85.00 videotape purchase)

Behavior Modification Technology
P.O. Box 597
Libertyville, Illinois 60048

This is one of three films distributed by Behavior Modification Technology. This film shows how behavior modification procedures can be used to teach retarded children, as well as psychotic children, to play games and socially interact.

*Teaching the mentally retarded: A positive approach* (1967, 22 minutes, black-and-white, 16mm., sound, free rental)

Dept. H.E.W.
National Medical Audio-Visual Center Annex
Station K
Atlanta, Georgia 30324

This film shows self-help therapy sessions over many months with retarded children. Emphasis is on the use of positive reinforcement in developing such skills as independent dressing and independent eating.

*Time out: A way to help children behave better* (n.d., black-and-white, 16mm., $21.00 two-day rental, $175.00 purchase)

Behavior Technics, Inc.
Box 116
Lemont, Pennsylvania 16851

This film teaches rules for using the time out behavior modification procedure to reduce unwanted behavior. Examples are given from a wide range of situations and ages. Emphasis is on reinforcement, not punishment as a preferred strategy. Time out rules are taught throughout the film—for example, "use immediately," "tell the child the behavior you want."

*Who did what to whom?* (1972, 16½ minutes, color, 16mm., sound, $195.00 purchase)

Research Press Company
Box 3177
Country Fair Station
Champaign, Illinois 61820

This film can *only* be purchased outright (though the film may be rented for a 3-day period for $25.00 in advance of purchase). The film comes with a Leader Guide and consists of 40 short scenes representing typical events which take place in the home, school, and office. Some scenes show children, some depict only adults, and others utilize both children and adults. The film helps the observer learn to recognize four principles of learning: positive reinforcement, negative reinforcement, extinction, and punishment. Although the film is short, with the discussion time that is alloted between each scene there is enough material for a two-hour session. Upon request, the distributor will send a free preview brochure.

# Selected Listing
# of Apparatus
# and Equipment Used
# in Behavior Modification
# With Children

# Selected Listing of Apparatus and Equipment Used in Behavior Modification With Children

*The apparatus and equipment listed here are frequently used in the behavior modification treatment of children. Where possible, the address of the distributor or the psychological journal reference (these journals are available at most professional libraries) accompanies each listing. Many of these items can also be purchased commercially or constructed on one's own.*

BUG-IN-THE-EAR SYSTEMS

These systems allow one person (e.g., a therapist) to communicate privately with one or more individuals (e.g., patient and/or parent) during a particular therapy or training session. The apparatus is ideal, for example, for giving immediate feedback to a parent, teacher, or therapy aide within the therapy situation—without distracting the patient or interrupting the therapy process.

Three relatively inexpensive systems have been developed. Each has its own advantages and each uses wires.

Morris, R. J. An inexpensive, easily built "bug-in-the-ear"/intercom system for training therapists in behavior modification techniques. *Behavior Therapy*, 1974, *5*, 685–686.

Stumphauzer, J. A low cost "bug-in-the-ear" sound system for modification of therapist, parent, and patient behavior. *Behavior Therapy*, 1971, *2*, 249–250.

Weathers, L., & Liberman, R. P. The Porta-Prompter—a new electronic prompting and feedback device: A technical note. *Behavior Therapy*, 1973, *4*, 703–705.

Another system is wireless but is also more expensive. For information, write to: Farrall Instrument Company, Grand Island, Nebraska 68801

COUNTERS

Counters (often called "digital counters") are very frequently used to count a wide variety of things and children's behaviors. For example, counters are used to count the number of rewards given per day, week, or session; the number of times a child performs a desirable or undesirable behavior per day, week, or session; and the number of points or tokens that a child accumulates per day, week or session (which are then exchanged for rewards). Counters come with single or multiple channels. The advantage of multiple channels is that the therapy aide, teacher, clinician, or parent can record the occurrence of more than one behavior or "thing" on the same machine. A counter should be reliable (i.e., register a "count" each time the mechanism is pressed), be error and trouble free, and be easy to operate.

A single-channel counter which looks and operate like commercially available golf counters can be purchased from:

>Behavior Research Company
>Box 3351
>Kansas City, Kansas 66103

A multiple-channel (5 channels) counter is available from:

>Lafayette Radio and Electronics
>111 Jericho Turnpike
>Syosset, L.I., New York 11791

## CHARTING EQUIPMENT

Charts are most often used to present graphically the occurrence of a particular behavior, providing the therapy agent with a graphic description of the progress of a child's treatment. Charts are also used, for example, to record the number of rewards per session a child receives.

Besides graph paper (like that presented in Appendix C), most charting equipment is electrically operated. The chart paper moves at a fixed speed. Connected to the paper is an ink pen which records a straight line as time progresses. When the pen is electrically activated by a switch held by the therapy agent, a small mark is recorded at a right angle to the line. Some equipment records each mark in a cumulative fashion (called a "cumulative recorder"), a second pen moving higher and higher each time a response is recorded. Once the pen reaches the top of the chart, it automically resets and returns to the bottom of the chart—moving up again each time it is activated.

Other equipment records each response on only one pen (called an "event recorder"). Here, the pen also records on a straight line as time progresses. When a response is recorded, the pen moves a very short distance away from the line and then back. More complex charting equipment, such as multipurpose polygraph machines like those used for recording electroencephalograms and electrocardiograms, are also available. For more information on charting equipment, write:

Lafayette Instrument Company
Box 1279
Lafayette, Indiana 47902
*or*
Esterline Angus
Box 2400
Indianapolis, Indiana 46224

## LIQUID DISPENSERS

Often in behavior modification work, it is necessary to reward a child with a liquid refreshment. The question which then arises is, "How should I dispense this liquid?" Some therapists use a plastic straw in a juice glass or soda glass. Others pour the child's refreshment portion in a small glass and have the child drink from the glass each time. Still others use a plastic dispenser for liquids which has a long spout. The liquid comes out of the spout each time the container is squeezed. In this way, the child receives his refreshment directly from the therapist, and the therapist has better control over how much goes into the child's mouth. This type of container, as well as others, is available commercially.

## PORTABLE TIMERS

Timers are often very important in behavior modification work. Timing the length of a particular therapy session, timing the length of time between observation periods, knowing how much time has elapsed since the last reward was delivered, timing how long a child is in a time out situation, and knowing how much time has passed since you last gave the child an instruction or fed or "checked up" on him are some very important ways that a timer is used in behavior modification therapy. Timers can also be used to help children understand the concept of time — e.g., elapsed time, how long a minute is versus 15 minutes, 30 minutes, and one hour.
　One such timer is the Memo-Timer, distributed by:
Charles Alshuler Company
Box 3720
Milwaukee, Wisconsin 53217
　Others (such as kitchen timers and parking meter timers) are available commercially in hardware and department stores. Another useful

timer is a commercially available stopwatch with either a 30-minute or a 60-minute cycle.

The obvious limitation of each of these timers is the length of time that they record, namely, 5–60 minutes. Few will record longer than 60 minutes. Another limitation is their loudness. When in operation, they are often noisy, and such noise can provide the child with potential cues about, for example, forthcoming rewards.

More expensive electromechanical and electronic (generally very quiet) timers are also available. For further information on these timers write:

BRS/LVE, Inc.
5301 Holland Drive
Beltsville, Maryland 20705

*or*

Lafayette Instrument Company
Box 1279
Lafayette, Indiana 47902

## TIME OUT AREAS

Often, it is difficult to establish a suitable time out room or area for a child. The room is occasionally too big or too small, too cluttered with distracting toys and objects, or too far away to be used promptly. The commercially available (Sears, Roebuck) three-panelled screen discussed in the following reference can be used as a suitable time out room: Harris, S., Ersner Hershfield, R., Carr Kaffashan, L., and Romanczyk, R. G. The portable time-out room. *Behavior Therapy*, 1974, *5*, 687–688. Its advantage is that it is both small and portable. Modified "do-it-yourself" versions can also be easily constructed.

## TOILET-TRAINING DEVICES

One behavior problem which parents, teachers, therapy aides, and clinicians often have difficulty solving is a child's lack of bladder and bowel control. Often, attempts at modifying the child's behavior are filled with anxiety, confusion, ignorance, and inconsistency—leading in many cases to the child's not being trained and the therapist's giving up for at least a while.

A number of devices have been discussed, but three which have received a good deal of attention are the following:

One apparatus which can be used for urine training children on the toilet (called "Potty Alert") as well as detecting when the children are wet away from the toilet (called "Pants Alert") is available from:

BRS/LVE, Inc.
5301 Holland Drive
Beltsville, Maryland 20705

See also: Kahinsky, W. Two low cost micturation alarms. *Behavior Therapy*, 1974, *5*, 698–700.

A second toilet-training device (called the Mark II Toilet Trainer) for alerting therapy agents when the child has wet his pants is distributed by:

Psytec
P.O. Box 26006
Tempe, Arizona 85281

A third device can be used at night for detecting if the child has wet his bed and for training him/her in bladder control. This apparatus is distributed commercially through Sears, Roebuck and Company and Montgomery Ward, Inc.

Another device for enuresis control has been described in: Fried, R. A device for enuresis control. *Behavior Therapy,* 1974, *5*, 682–684. It is small, inexpensive to build, and can be used, as can the previous devices, within a behavior modification program.

One procedure for bowel training children (in particular, retarded children) has been outlined in a book by Richard M. Foxx and Nathan H. Azrin called *Toilet training the retarded* (see reference in Suggested Additional Readings section).

OTHER EQUIPMENT

Other equipment which has been used in behavior modification work— mainly in conjunction with training therapists (or giving feedback to therapists)—are the following:

1. *Audio tape recorders*: either reel-to-reel or cassette tape recorders
2. *Video tape recorders*: either portable battery operated or stationary video recorders; both color and black-and-white systems are available
3. *Movie cameras*: available in 8mm., Super 8, or 16mm. Sound can be recorded on some Super 8 and most 16mm. movie cameras; film is available for both color and black-and-white movies

Further information about this equipment is available from most commercial instrumentation and photography companies.

Additional information regarding equipment used in behavior modification treatment is available from the following sources:

BRS/LVE
5301 Holland Drive
Beltsville, Maryland 20705

Lafayette Instrument Company
Box 1279
Lafayette, Indiana 47902

Farrall Instrument Company
P.O. Box 1037
Grand Island, Nebraska 68801

*appendix* **G**

# Suggested
# Additional Readings

# Suggested Additional Readings

Ayllon, T., & Azrin, N. H. *The token economy: A motivational system for therapy and rehabilitation.* New York: Appleton-Century-Crofts, 1968.

Bandura, A. *Principles of behavior modification.* New York: Holt, Rinehart and Winston, 1969.

Becker, W. C. *Parents are teachers.* Champaign, Ill.: Research Press, 1971.

Browning, R. M., & Stover, D. O. *Behavior modification in child treatment: An experimental and clinical approach.* Chicago: Aldine-Atherton, 1970.

Ferster, C. B., & Perrott, M. D. *Behavior principles.* New York: Appleton-Century-Crofts, 1968.

Foxx, R. M. & Azrin, N. H. *Toilet training the retarded.* Champaign, Ill.: Research Press, 1973.

Gardner, W. I. *Behavior modification: Applications in mental retardation.* Chicago: Aldine-Atherton, 1971.

Gelfand, D. M. *Social learning in childhood.* Belmont, Calif.: Brooks/Cole, 1969.

Graziano, A. M. *Child without tomorrow.* New York: Pergamon Press, 1974.

Kanfer, F. H., & Phillips, J. S. *Learning foundations of behavior therapy.* New York: John Wiley & Sons, 1970.

Karen, R. L. *An introduction to behavior theory and its applications.* New York: Harper & Row, 1974.

Krumboltz, J. D., & Krumboltz, H. B. *Changing children's behavior.* Englewood Cliffs, N.J.: Prentice-Hall, 1972.

Madsen, C. H., Jr., & Madsen, C. K. *Teaching/Discipline: A positive approach for educational development* (2nd ed.). Boston: Allyn & Bacon, 1974.

Neisworth, J. T., & Smith, R. M. *Modifying retarded behavior.* Boston: Houghton Mifflin, 1973.

Patterson, G. R., & Guillon, M. E. *Living with children.* Champaign, Ill.: Research Press, 1968.

Quay, H. C., & Werry, J. S. *Psychopathological disorders of childhood.* New York: John Wiley & Sons, 1972.

Rimm, D. C., & Masters, J. C. *Behavior therapy: Theoretical and empirical findings.* New York: Academic Press, 1974.

Ross, A. O. *Psychological disorders of children.* McGraw-Hill, 1974.

Skinner, B. F. *Science and human behavior.* New York: Macmillan, 1953.

Tharp, R. G., & Wetzel, R. J. *Behavior modification in the natural environment.* New York: Academic Press, 1969.

Watson, L. S., Jr. *Child behavior modification.* New York: Pergamon Press, 1973.

Whaley, D. L., & Malott, R. W. *Elementary principles of behavior.* New York: Appleton-Century-Crofts, 1971.

*The following books contain a collection of research studies and/or theoretical articles on behavior modification with children:*

Ashem, B. A., & Poser, E. G. (Eds.). *Adaptive learning: Behavior modification with children.* New York: Pergamon Press, 1973.

Graziano, A. M. (Ed.). *Behavior therapy with children.* Chicago: Aldine-Atherton, 1971, 1975. (2 vols.)

Lovaas, I. O., & Bucher, B. D. (Eds.). *Perspectives in behavior modification with deviant children.* Englewood Cliffs, N.J.: Prentice-Hall, 1974.

O'Leary, K. D., & O'Leary, S. G. *Classroom management: The successful use of behavior modification.* New York: Pergamon Press, 1972.

Thompson, T., & Grabowski, J. (Eds.). *Behavior modification of the mentally retarded.* New York: Oxford University Press, 1972.

Ulrich, R., Stachnik, T., & Mabry, J. (Eds.). *Control of human behavior,* Vol. 3. Glenview, Ill.: Scott, Foresman, 1974.

# Index